Contents

Introduction   1

1   Leading a drama group   3

2   Ways of approaching work   6
    Encouraging concentration and focus   8
    Movement   21
    Movement developing from verbal suggestions   22
    Movement developing from vocal sounds   29
    Movement developing from percussion   32
    Poetry and song as a stimulus for movement   34
    Developing abstract interpretations of a theme   35
    Developing a character, or becoming someone else   40
    Role-play   51
    Games   55
    Evaluation   59

3   Material for improvisation   61
    Choosing a topic   61
    The initial approach   62
    Story-telling   64
    Group story-telling   68
    Story-telling material   74
    Poems   76
    Theme work   81
    Situations   83

4   Space and equipment   87
    A room of your own   87
    Equipment   90
    Materials   91
    Costume   93
    Masks   94
    Creating simple sets   101
    Props   105
    The audience   106

5   Preparing for a production   109
    Choice of topic and audience   110
    Preparation and rehearsal   114
    Structure of the programme and sequence of items   116
    Costume, set, props, lighting   118
    Final rehearsals   120

6   Synopses of some improvised productions   123

Appendices
    The Story of Peter, Paul and Espen   132
    The Butterdish   135

Book List   136

Films   138

Acknowledgments   139

Drama fulfils man's need to play and to create. The dramatic activity will include exploration with others – through the imagination and the intellect, the mind and the body – of the real world and the imaginary. Through drama man may come to terms with his experience. The uniqueness of the activity is that he may achieve this in a group – drama is social, where many other arts are not – and it does not necessarily depend upon any identifiable skill or technique. Often it deals with those situations where words fail.

The essential ingredient of drama is that experience should be gained at the same sort of time-scale as occurs in life. It involves the participant as himself or in a role, being obliged to make decisions which will move the action forward to an as yet unexplored area.

Reproduced, by permission, from *Examinations in Drama*, an occasional bulletin issued by the English Committee of the Schools Council, London (summer 1974).

Drama without Script
the practice of improvised drama

Susan M. Stanley

HODDER AND STOUGHTON
LONDON SYDNEY AUCKLAND TORONTO

Line illustrations by Kate Buxton

British Library Cataloguing in Publication Data

Stanley, Susan M
    Drama without script.
    1. Drama in education
    2. Improvisation (Acting)
    I. Title
    792'.028   PN3171

ISBN 0 340 23768 6 Unibook

First published 1980
Copyright © 1980 Susan M. Stanley

Set, printed and bound in Great Britain for
Hodder and Stoughton Educational,
a division of Hodder and Stoughton Ltd,
Mill Road, Dunton Green, Sevenoaks, Kent,
by Fakenham Press Limited, Fakenham, Norfolk

Introduction

'Man only plays when in the full meaning of the word he is a man, and he is only completely a man when he plays.' (Schiller)

This book is about the kind of drama which does not depend upon a playwright for its existence but which develops from the involvement of those taking part in it. I have not written about how to act, or how to produce a formal play; my object is to provide a framework for those who are interested in a more spontaneous way of working. Individuals cannot effectively go off and improvise drama situations on their own. For constructive work a group of people is required and, as with all groups, there must be a leader. This book is thus written primarily, though not exclusively, for potential leaders and teachers of drama workshop groups who want to explore the possibilities of improvisation and develop their own personal approach to the work.

Improvised drama can give people unlimited scope to express ideas and feelings and to make fullest use of mind, body and imagination. Working with a group over a period of time will help them to develop self-confidence and a deeper awareness and understanding of each other's point of view, and, as their mutual trust and sensitivity increase, the natural barriers to communication—shyness, self-consciousness, diffidence—will be eliminated. Through improvised situations a group can explore character and situations of conflict, probe problems and gain insight into the way human beings are motivated. Individuals can be helped towards a maturity of personal expression and fluency of communication that would be unattainable in the course of traditional drama club work, which tends to favour the extrovert.

The methods and ideas given in this book have been used with a variety of age groups and will be of equal value for children, young people and adults. They include exercises for experimenting in unusual ways with movement, sound, abstract themes, stories and poems, role play and character, as well as suggestions for creating simple sets and costumes. I must stress, however, that I do not believe these exercises are of any value to the group meeting for a limited number of weeks for the sole purpose of 'putting on a play'. A performance, however small the audience, is to some extent an examination of the teacher's and the group's dramatic abilities, and as a result the pressures of a formal scripted production can stifle creative growth and inhibit the development of the group spirit. But when a group works regularly over a prolonged period its members will learn to explore spontaneously and imaginatively together, and may become so stimulated and so enthusiastic about the outcome of some of their work that they want to share these recently discovered ideas with other people. By this time, too, the teacher or leader has gained confidence in the role of co-ordinator rather than director.

An unscripted production gives the group members considerable freedom of expression and allows them to share the various responsibilities, each being in turn actor, producer, designer, song-writer, costume and props maker, lighting controller, and so on. Everyone is encouraged to contribute and decisions are made in consultation with the leader. This process of achieving a group statement through drama, without playwright or script, is thus a satisfying and enjoyable experience for everyone concerned. Response from an audience can add an extra dimension of pleasure to the work, and audiences may also find that they are jolted into a more active role when they find themselves involved in the unexpected, whether it comes through the action, the resourceful use of costume and sets, or the overall exuberance of a united group who are committed to the success of their *own* work.

1 Leading a drama group

If you are interested in leading or teaching a drama group, do not be put off by the fact that you may have no formal drama training. Many people have become very competent drama teachers without any experience of the theatre. You will, however, require plenty of initiative, imagination, enthusiasm and tact, and you will need to be the kind of person who enjoys commitment to a challenge but also has a sense of perspective, and who is prepared to recognise that while the work should be fun it must remain under control if it is to succeed.

A drama session starts to 'work' as soon as you begin to tune into the mood of your group and to find your own way of encouraging its members to develop spontaneously the material that is being used; in this way they will be extended and will gain a sense of immediate achievement. You must learn to assess the particular needs of your group and decide what your objectives will be, both within a session and over a period of time.

If you are genuinely interested in listening to and respecting the ideas and opinions of those in your group, no matter what their ages, you will rapidly gain their confidence and co-operation, and the resulting exchange of thoughts and ideas will lead to existing discoveries. You will find, too, that it is often worth relinquishing your own pre-conceived ideas for a more appropriate alternative offered by someone in the group. A variety of approaches may be necessary (see Chapters 2 and 3) to start the ball rolling and help the group explore a topic so that it becomes illuminated in a new way. Gradually a climate of trust will be created within which you can all work together generously and sensitively.

Sometimes group members will work in a controlled and concentrated way, absorbed in what they are doing and at the same time thoroughly enjoying their explorations. Now and again the quality of the involvement and the emotion arising from it will cause their disbelief to be suspended in such a way that there will be an extraordinary sense of oneness within the group; they will momentarily have transcended the make-believe and reached an imagined reality. At other times nothing will be created during a session and unless you suggest an alternative way of working it may end in confusion.

As you gain confidence, try to develop the habit of looking at the outcome of a session or a series of sessions in an objective but analytical way. Was it a success, and if so, why? If the group did not respond, what was the reason? In this way you can assess development and decide on the most appropriate approach for the next session. Always have various alternative plans up your sleeve in case your original idea does not suit the general mood, and be prepared to adapt your method, too, if your own mood changes just before a session.

Planning the content of the work

When planning an improvised drama course and considering what material to use, an awareness of the particular interests and abilities of the group is necessary. With young children up to the age of six, the length of the session must be short to start with and can be gradually extended as they become more involved in the work. Time, patience and good humour are of paramount importance. For children between the ages of seven and about thirteen years, the drama method is mainly concerned with skills, group awareness and exploring the imagination. As the children develop emotionally, intellectually and socially, it is more concerned with the extension of thought and feeling through group questioning. Young people and adults will become involved in the dimensions of a problem and with gaining deeper insight into character, using speech, movement, thought and questioning. This gives them the opportunity to develop personality, adaptability and a flexible attitude to everyday problems.

It is worth planning to include some of the following approaches in each block of sessions, so that the group becomes familiar with experience of various kinds:

For children up to thirteen—stretch their imagination so that places, characters and events are created from a bare room, using only body movement and voice; encourage awareness of the different ways of expressing ideas, by active experiment rather than discussion; select a focus, such as exercises and games, situations, stories and poems, character work, to be developed gradually and supplemented with mask making, puppetry, painting and writing which may evolve from the session; use annual events such as Christmas or Hallowe'en, or local customs. Group plays and scenes are valid but need a motivated context. Never let the session turn into a routine of

small groups producing static little 'plays' which go on for ever
—this is not drama but a soft option for both teacher and class.

Bear in mind that during the first few meetings children may feel
self-conscious in front of you and one another and find it difficult to
'suspend disbelief' during an imaginative exercise. A certain
amount of straight-forward task work such as described in the
movement exercises in Chapter 2 will help, and all the children
should be encouraged to join in.

For young people and adults—if the initial groundwork has been
covered in previous years, then groups will be capable of working in
depth on topics related to their experience and interests. Otherwise,
they will need the chance to relate to one another, acquire essential
skills and stimulate their imaginations so that they can respond
spontaneously. They are then ready for provoking and pertinent
questioning about the work in hand. Through questioning you can
deepen their insight and perception about people and situations.
Unless there is good reason, try not to accept the trite response or
stock characterisation; demand quality of thought and you will find
that most groups will respond. Challenge them if you feel they can
contribute more, but remember that encouragement is a stimulant.

Focus on topics such as development of character—conflict
within a character or between different characters, identification
with character traits; shape of plot—logical sequence of ideas moving towards juxtaposition of ideas; abstract work, portraying an idea
symbolically in movement and sound; interpreting ideas through
different media, e.g. tape-recorder, camera, projector, lights;
creating environments from waste materials; exploring the relationship of audience, set and actors. Some ideas can be explored
through fantasy, using visual and vocal means of expression; others
need to be probed more realistically, exploring theme as well as plot.

The suggestions I have outlined here are described more fully in the
following pages, and will, I hope, provide a foundation for the
aspiring drama workshop leader and teacher and perhaps a source
of fresh ideas for those who have already some experience.

2 Ways of approaching work

There are many ways of starting a drama session. This chapter is divided into sections so that you can experiment with the various exercises suggested, changing and adapting them to suit yourself and the needs of the group you are working with. 'The needs of the group' is an ambiguous phrase to someone new to drama teaching, so how do you ascertain what they are likely to be? I am making a huge generalisation by saying that there are roughly four different group-types to be considered. In fact, every group has a personality peculiar to itself. Yours will probably fall between several of these categories, and will gradually adopt and invent a pattern of work which suits both you and itself. I usually experiment with various starting points until I find something which draws us all together so that there is an overall feeling of excitement and elation. We are then sufficiently inspired to invent and create together, and at the end of the session we feel a warm sense of satisfaction and can look back with shared amusement at our initial struggles.

The four group-types tend to be:

1 Bubbly and energetic—this type quite often enjoys games or exercises which channel energy and encourage sensitivity to self and one another.
2 Diffident, quiet and self-conscious—this type needs lively games and exercises to encourage the loss of inhibitions, and others which encourage concentration and spontaneity.
3 Perverse and unable to work together—unless members of a group are able to integrate, there is little hope that they will be able to create. Try using games in which they have to decide the rules and keep to them. If they are sufficiently interested in the enjoyment of the game they will not welcome disruptive influences. Games and exercises demanding energy are often worth using initially. Discussion on topics they suggest is helpful as ideas are shared, argued about and in time modified.
4 Unimaginative, happy to be directed and spoon-fed—the members of this group probably need reassurance, as they are insecure and afraid to expose their ideas either to you or to one another. I have never yet met a group who were completely unimaginative or lacking in spontaneity; it may take months to reassure them that their ideas are valid, but eventually they will learn to share

and enjoy them. Choose exercises and games which are immediately successful, so that people become receptive to the work. Then select exercises which help to unblock the imagination—for instance, ones in which the player does not predecide what the outcome will be but allows something to happen. (It is understood between class and teacher that sometimes nothing happens and sometimes there is a surprising happening—both negative and positive results can be expected in any session.)

The exercises in this chapter are primarily concerned with stimulating groups to work spontaneously and in a sustained way. Your aim is to encourage them to produce their own ideas and themes which they want to explore, and then help them to explore these in depth so that you get away from the trite statement to one which has evolved from a joint creative effort. The role of the teacher is as a balance for the group, to help them through indulgent, intense sessions towards work which expresses accurately what they want to show or say. You need to develop 'antennae' which sense and respond to the many moods of the group, and at the same time you will gradually build up a stock of different ways of probing and solving such problems as starting a tricky session, changing an atmosphere, and so on.

Warm-up exercises

Encouraging concentration and focus

The exercises described below are useful for encouraging concentration and body control. Some are good for individual work, and others help the group to work together freely and without embarrassment. I find they provide personal as well as group stability and are a useful lead into imaginative work. They are not, however, suitable for a difficult and energetic group to start on; for that type I usually select a vigorous game.

Sequence 1—Listening to sounds

'When I tell you to, and not before, move into a space on your own and stand there without touching anyone. Stand very still, balance yourself between your toes and heels, arms hanging loosely by your side. Let's see how many people can manage the exercise without opening their eyes. Please shut your eyes and listen to the sounds I suggest to you.'

You could then ask the group to listen to the various sounds outside the room, noting the type of sound and what may cause it. Then try sounds within the room, emphasising that no extra sounds should be added. Finally, tell them to listen to and become aware of the movement of their own breathing. They can then open their eyes slowly. You might like to check how many people were able to get through the exercise without opening their eyes. Let there be an element of competition each time you try the exercise. Discuss the sounds that were heard—heavy sounds outside, such as a lorry trundling past; or light sounds within the room, such as a clock ticking. Let the class evaluate the degree of overall concentration.

Extension   Tell the group to shut their eyes again and listen to one sound made by you. They should be encouraged to imagine what the sound could represent rather than how it was made. You might make a gentle, rhythmic tapping with a pencil; responses to this sound might include a branch against a window pane, a dripping roof, a blind man walking down a street. Then ask for volunteers to make a sound. Let them experiment one at a time, keeping the sound simple but repeating it several times until you ask the group to open their eyes. This can be developed in many ways. Smaller groups may be formed to make up a sound pattern together, which can then be taped. The taped 'sound-music' may then be played to the whole group as a stimulus for movement or improvisation.

Sequence 2—Moving to a point

Again the group should be well spaced out and standing apart from each other. As this is a very positive exercise to encourage focus and concentration, the instructions which are given must be very clear. Each member of the group should look for a spot on the floor a few feet away from where he or she is standing, to which he will move when told to begin. His eyes must not wander from the point. Movement must be direct and very slow and simple; the feeling of slowness must be *felt*. Ask each group member to wait very quietly when he reaches his point, as the exercise does not finish until they have all completed the move. If some start off too fast, stop them all and re-emphasise the original instructions—SLOW, SILENT, SIMPLE. Encourage them all to repeat this exercise once or twice, then try to stimulate them into seeing an image on the spot towards which they are slowly moving. Encourage them to see the image while they are moving; there is no need for them to plan in advance what the image is to be, as the point of the exercise is to unblock the imagination. If you try this exercise several times yourself, you will find that sometimes you see an image—it might be an object, an animal, an atmosphere—sometimes you only see the point you are moving to. Emphasise to the group that the quality of the image is more important than the quantity of images seen. The aim is to see and react to an imaginative image which is a surprise to the person seeing it, and which is so clear that it is describable. An inhibited group may take some time to achieve this, so leave the exercise and return to it another time. Do not force the group to think out an imagined object; they should let the image appear spontaneously as they are moving towards the spot. I always give lots of encouragement and show that I am thoroughly delighted as people begin to respond more precisely and spontaneously to this exercise.

Extension The same amount of initial focus on a selected point must be encouraged; the point can be on the floor, at eye level, or even higher. Then everyone in his own time moves directly or indirectly (but *very quickly*) and responds to the point on which his concentration has been focused. Again encourage the group to imagine spontaneous images.

This exercise could be developed in various ways: for instance, the quick movement might be followed by a slow movement, letting the contrast of speed be the main objective; or a quick sound could be added to accompany the quick movement and a slow sound to accompany the slow movement; work on a sound and movement sequence could then follow.

Sequence 3—Exploring the area without moving from the spot

Members of the group should be standing apart from each other. Tell them that each must explore the whole area around his own body and see how much territory he has within stretching distance of the spot on which he is standing; how high and how low he can reach, how far forward, how far to the back and to the right and left. Encourage each one to explore the area as fully as possible, particularly the floor. The exercise aims to limber up different parts of the body within this given area. Only one part of the body should be moved at a time (one leg, the tongue, one shoulder, one eye). Suggest that a large part of the body and a small part are moved alternatively. The different parts should be moved very slowly or very quickly, and the level of movement should be changed continually; for instance, bend the lower leg very slowly towards the floor, freeze in that position, and follow this large, slow movement by throwing the head backwards very fast.

Encourage variety of level and precise movement at speed, limbering up the whole body.

When the group seems quite at ease, suggest that a small sound be added to accompany the movement but that it must be a sound appropriate to the size and speed of the movement—a slow sound

Warm-up exercises

with a slow movement, a quick sound with a quick movement. In addition, the sound could be low if the movement is at floor level, high or strong if the movement is up high. Encourage this co-ordination of sound with movement and stress that at all times there must be total personal involvement and concentration; individuals should not be aware of one another.

Extension—filmstrip Tell the class that they will initially be depicting a still from a filmstrip. Let them start by doing the exercise described above, then ask them to freeze and tell them the subject of the film. Then tell them that the film will start to move very slowly, and that they must develop the action of the film from the precise position they were frozen in for the still until they are working at normal speed. Once they have completed the film sequence, they return to the basic exercise. Freeze them several times and suggest various subjects, but sometimes encourage them to think up their own films from the positions in which they are frozen.

Subjects for filmstrip action could include the following:

spring cleaning	gardening on an allotment
mending a car	window dressing
tailor or dressmaker at work	decorating a room
feeding birds	a scientist at work
a street seller	part of a machine,
a plumber at work	working on a machine
laying the table	making a spell
taking a cow to market	workmen on a building site
a pickpocket at work	an animal in a cage
looking for a lost contact lens	

Any of these ideas may be developed into a group improvisation, particularly those which naturally involve a team or group such as workmen on a building site, part of a machine, gardening on an allotment. Many more topics will come to mind as you talk to the group.

A further extension of this idea would be a filmstrip worked in pairs, A and B. Each pair carries out the exercise on page 10, moving parts of the body slowly and quickly on the spot. When told to freeze, A considers the position he is in and relates it to B, and then starts to mime a situation arising from his position and if possible related to B's. B holds his position, watches A, and then responds to A's actions. Suggest that as the mime works itself to a conclusion each reverts to the slow/quick abstract actions. On the next freeze it is B's turn to consider the situation and decide on the mimed action.

Sequence 4—Looking

The group should stand well spaced out. The aim is to focus on a selected point in the room when a signal is given. The focus must be very decisive. Start by beating out a good, firm rhythm on a drum or a metal waste-paper bin: e.g.'One—two—three—*freeze!*' The group move to the drum beat and at 'freeze' all point to and look at an exact spot, with arm extended and the whole body focused on the point they are looking at. They must also say the word 'LOOK!' loudly and clearly. Suggest that they focus on things behind them, to the side, and so on. Invent and develop the exercise as you will.

An amusing extension is to get the group to point at one another, and to alter the tonal quality of 'Look', saying it in a whisper, or with inflections of surprise, fear, amusement, or other emotions. This is a good exercise for a group to start off with, and it can lead into all kinds of interesting variations.

Sequence 5—Mirror exercises

Excellent for concentration and sensitivity when working with a partner. Divide the group into pairs, facing one another. Each pair stands, kneels or sits in identical positions, arms preferably at sides (but you may develop the exercise as it becomes more familiar). A starts, very slowly moving one hand followed by the arm. B copies A's movement so exactly that it should not be apparent who is leading. As skill and confidence increase, other parts of the body are used. A should have the opportunity to follow B, and after a while they should be encouraged to give and take the leadership, letting it pass gradually from one to the other and back again as movement continues and concentrating on precise tracing of each other's movements. This is an exercise involving equality rather than dominance.

Extension A makes a specific, realistic action (e.g. shaving, making-up) and B simultaneously repeats the movement (slow motion is advisable for inexperienced partners). It is important that the leader judges the pace of the movement so that each appears to be precisely mirroring the other.

As a further development, A can mime a character in the process of, for example, preparing to go out for an evening, and B simultaneously mirrors the action and the facial mannerisms.

When working in groups of four, both the As perform the action, the Bs act as the reflection. The sequence might portray a barber's

shop, or reflections in a shop window. Encourage identical, simul-
taneous movement and slow-motion action.

Sequence 6—Copying

Pair off the group again. Partners should stand opposite one another
in a neutral position with hands by their sides. A is to teach B a
simple movement, such as how to raise an arm, bend a hand, and so
on. A makes the movement and freezes into the final position. B
watches and, when A has finished, B repeats the movement as
precisely as possible. Encourage simple movements and accurate
observation. Note, too, that in this exercise the pair do not move
simultaneously, as with mirror work. Let B take over the leadership
before extending this exercise.

Extension With A as the puppet master and B as the puppet or
dummy, the same routine of movement takes place, but this time A
builds up a sequence of simple movements—with a freeze in
between each stage of the sequence so that B can copy during the
pause. As an example, A might show B how to sit down, walk, drink
a cup of tea, or perform similar actions.

Sequence 7—Dubbing

Now that A or B can control his partner/puppet and teach him to
move, he can begin to teach him to talk as well. Starting as master, A
makes a sound. B listens and copies the precise pitch and tone of the
sound. Let them experiment for a little, then suggest that A utters a
word and gradually progresses to a phrase, while B listens and
repeats each word, again copying pitch and tone. B then becomes
master and teaches A—sound, word, phrase, and finally sentence.

I have found that people with reading problems have very much
enjoyed this exercise and have shown a surprising facility for
remembering and repeating precisely a long piece of dialogue made
up of several complicated sentences.

Extension The pairs now join up into groups of four. In this part of
the exercise the masters provide the dialogue, which the puppets
repeat exactly, and the puppets provide movement to fit in with the
dialogue. The As (masters) sit facing the Bs, who position themselves in a 'frozen' picture. A^1 speaks, B^1 repeats exactly, A^2
responds and B^2 repeats the response and moves accordingly.
Slowly a situation evolves. Let both As and Bs have an equal amount

of time and opportunity to explore each role.

When a group is beginning to be familiar with a script, dubbing is a useful way of helping them to learn lines. They are not hindered by a book and therefore have freedom of movement, as well as having to exercise a certain amount of concentration in remembering and repeating the dialogue. For a further extension of this section, see the suggestions for work with masks, pages 98, 100.

Sequence 8—Exercises to encourage listening

A useful game involving the whole group divided into two teams is played sitting in a circle. Team 1 sits on the left of the teacher in a semi-circle, and the circle is completed by Team 2 on the teacher's right. The teacher whispers the same message into the ear of the two people sitting next to him. Each of them repeats the message in a whisper to his neighbour, who listens and whispers it to the next person. The team which has the most accurate rendering of the original message is the winner.

Variation   One person stands in the centre of the circle, the rest stand round holding hands. A message is passed by hand movement round the circle and the person in the centre must guess where the message is. Alternatively, someone stands blindfold in the centre of the circle, and this time the message is whispered round the circle and the blind man must either point to where the whisper is or touch the people who are giving and receiving the message.

Extension   In pairs, with A and B sitting opposite one another. A tells B how he travelled to work that day, or what happened from the moment he woke up. B listens, and has to repeat the information in the third person.

Variations   A and B both talk at the same time, either as suggested above or perhaps telling a well-known fairy story. The object is for each to keep on with his own account and not to let himself be interrupted or made to pause or hesitate by the person opposite.

A and B talk to each other but they are not allowed to say 'yes' or 'no'. See which pair can keep talking the longest, or let one person be challenged by the rest of the class.

Extension   Again in pairs; this exercise is particularly useful for a group who are inarticulate and afraid to use their imaginations. Start by telling them a story, either one imagined on the spur of the moment or an adaptation of a well-known one. All must listen carefully, because they do not know when you will stop and they do not know whether A or B will have to carry on telling the story to the other. This is an excellent way of encouraging the group to listen really attentively, and may be worked on in groups of four just as successfully. When you do stop, ask either As or Bs to carry on. Let them develop the action for a while and then say 'Change' and the other partners must pick up the story from that point.

Variation   In pairs. The teacher starts by speaking the dialogue of two different characters. If you are sufficiently confident, suggest that the class give you the names of two people or things they would like to hear in conversation. Exaggerate a vocal difference between the two characters. When you feel you have got the involvement of the group, pause and say that the As will now take over the first character and the Bs the second. They could first do this without any action, and at a later stage add movements.

Sequence 9—Still pictures

This requires two groups, As and Bs, and a large space between them, with perhaps a table or chair as a focal point. The As move one by one into the space and freeze into a position which they must be able to hold for a few minutes. They should be quite close together. Each member of the B group notes the shape of the 'picture' thus formed and then the exact position of his opposite number among the As, who must now shut his eyes. The Bs then gently lead the As away, until the whole picture has been dismantled; and then, in turn, take them (still with eyes closed) back to the centre and direct them verbally into their original positions until the 'picture' is created exactly as before. The As can then open their eyes and tell their partners if they are in the same position as at the start.

Variation   One of each pair manipulates his partner into a position or shape which can be held for up to five minutes. A subject can be given, such as statues in a park. The partner must remember his exact position, as he then has to put his manipulator into an identical one. This is a very good test of sensitivity; so often a position is chosen which cannot be held for longer than a minute or two without arms aching or legs quivering.

Extension   Use the whole group to depict a tableau. Let the group sit in a semi-circle; it helps if you have a few spare stools or tables available. Ask the group for suggestions for the tableau—for example, photographs at an exhibition, a surgical operation, an excavation; then call out the title. One by one, people move quickly into the space to form the tableau. Once there are sufficient people in it, you say 'Action', and they respond to each other either in mime or with added speech. Sometimes it is fun to have three groups: groups A and B make still pictures and group C guesses the title or titles of the pictures and asks for action to happen.

As a follow-up to this you might find it useful to bring in postcards or photographs of groups of people and get the class to re-form the positions of the people in them, and then ask for action; or to suggest that the photograph is the starting point for a scene. Alternatively, the scene might conclude with the whole class in the exact positions seen in the photograph. Encourage observation of the natural poses and the arrangement of groups of people; you will soon find that the movements of the class in relation to each other will become less static and more naturalistic and interesting.

Sequence 10—Giving and receiving presents

A pleasant, light-hearted exercise to encourage spontaneity, observation and unselfconsciousness when working with a partner. When the group is beginning to be fairly responsive and imaginative, say: 'Somewhere in this room there is a present for each of you. It is very small, round and heavy. It is hidden, please find it. Before you open it, note the colour of the wrapping paper, the sort of paper it is and how it is sealed. Unwrap the present gently and carefully, as you don't know what it is; the only hint is that it will be something that will please you.' While they are doing this, move around and ask people questions about where they found the present, how it is wrapped, and so on.

Next let them form pairs, preferably with unfamiliar partners. A gives B a present, a very nice present. Where does A find the present, which has been hidden? Is the present heavy or light? Large or small? What shape is it? A must indicate the size and shape by the way he holds it and gives it to B. B observes. On receiving the present, B imagines the colour and type of wrapping and seal, carefully undoes the parcel and then shows A what the present is by using it. No words need be spoken. B then goes off and finds his present to give to A in a similar way.

Contrast this with the suggestion that the partners give one another really nasty presents; for example, A picks a large, furry spider off the wall and puts it on to B, or B goes off to fill a bucket full of flour and then throws it all over A. Again they must guess what they are being given. The nasty presents can also be given as slyly as can be imagined.

Object simulation—unwrapping a parcel

Variation B wraps up A as a present—a very fragile present. B then becomes a present which A must unwrap. Stipulate that the present must be something not in human form, i.e. it cannot be a doll or a statue.

This exercise of giving and receiving presents is a good starter for a drama session and should be quite light-hearted in approach. It also works well after some of the previous exercises which require intense concentration.

Sequence 11—Changes

Suitable for a group who are responsive and work well together; it helps to encourage a spontaneous response to an unknown situation. The whole group sit in a semi-circle. An improvised set can be created from any odds and ends that are handy (chairs, boxes, an upside-down table, drapes, say). The set should be altered for each new change sequence. If the group is lively and uninhibited, let people respond spontaneously to the situation as the sequence progresses; if they are less likely to participate, give each person a number or letter.

The first person (A) who moves into the set must have no preconceived idea of who or where he might be. As he moves he must allow himself to become a character and the set to become a place, and he then performs some suitable action. It could be static (for example, standing and waiting quite passively), or he might start to clean the floor, or wash his hands under a tap, or sit with his back to the group. The next person to enter (B) develops the situation as he sees it. A must respond and relate to B, even though B interprets A differently from the way A had imagined himself. For instance, if A saw himself sitting in a doctor's surgery with a pain in his big toe, he must give up this idea when B greets him as a long-lost friend sitting in a cafe. More people then enter, one by one, and develop the scene created by A and B, keeping to the same situation.

As with all improvised situations, there comes a weakening point, and no more can be said to extend the action. The characters and their response to each other crumble. It is now up to the onlookers to change the situation. One person from the group goes in and says something which completely alters the place as well as the characterisation. The person who makes the change has the authority to indicate, in character, that so-and-so is needed elsewhere, so that one of the actors leaves the scene. The people already on the set must respond instantly by adopting a new, appropriate character, realising the new place and becoming part of the new situation. These changes should occur whenever the action crumbles. If the group are not good at participating without encouragement, give each member a number and then call out a number at random when the moment comes for a new character to enter the scene or change the situation. Encourage spontaneity of ideas, perceptive characterisation, clear mime, alacrity of takeover, and acute observation and attention to each other's words.

Variation—Exits and entrances.   The group stand in a semi-circle (this exercise works best with about fourteen people). People enter the circle in turn and mainly work on their own, in mime. As they enter, the movement must be definite, although the reason for moving in such a way need not be predetermined. In fact, the best ideas are those that spring from the way in which the movement is made. For instance, as someone moves into the space very slowly, backwards, he realises that an imaginary person is forcing him into a room; suddenly he jumps at his assailant, knocks him out and leaps out of the room—a clear entrance and a definite exit. Sometimes, when someone gets 'stuck' in the centre and cannot work out an exit, another person might help him by driving a car into the circle and giving him a lift.

Sequence 12—Using the senses to explore a room

Ask the group to have a good look round the room and try to notice any marks, sockets, ledges and so on which they had not been aware of before. We often become too familiar with a place, and fail to notice all sorts of distinguishing marks.

Ask the group to shut their eyes and listen to the sounds both inside and outside the room. Suggest they listen to sounds with an ear against the floor or close up to a wall. Talk about the variety of sounds heard.

Then suggest that all move round the room, touching as many different textures as they can find, and feeling the different temperatures of leather, wood, plastic, and so on. Ask them to find words to describe the feel of the different surfaces. Then suggest that they smell some of them, particularly those made of wood and fabric.

It is not, I'm afraid, practical to ask people to taste the room! I did once have a group who were responding so perfectly to the above suggestions that I said, very seriously, 'Now taste the surfaces you've already touched and smelt.' There was a pause and they all turned and looked at me to see if my tongue was really in my cheek.

Sequence 13—Blind exercises to encourage trust in someone else

Working in pairs, one partner (A) can see, the other (B) is 'blind' (encourage Bs to keep their eyes shut rather than use.a blindfold). A turns B around several times, so that his sense of direction is confused. A then gently leads B, perhaps holding him by the hand, to different areas of the room. A can change the pace as B becomes more confident, but he must never force B to move in a manner or a direction which is against his will. As the pairs get more proficient, place obstacles in the space, so that the sighted partner has to lead the blind man over them with the help of verbal instructions. This is more interesting if the obstacles are set after the blind man has shut his eyes. This exercise can also be extended out-of-doors; it is an illuminating experience to touch leaves and grass and smell flowers when one is in the 'blind' state. Encourage a high degree of trust between the partners, and reverse the roles frequently.

Variation The group should be evenly spaced out round the four walls of the room, with backs to the centre. The centre should be clear of all objects. Everyone should be facing the wall with his eyes shut before he starts to move. You then direct all to move towards the centre of the room in a certain way—for example, backwards on their knees, very slowly on all fours, turning a half-circle and moving to the left. When the majority are within reasonable distance of each other, suggest that they find out who is near them. They may *only* feel, with eyes still shut, and may touch only the face and head of the other person. They continue to investigate until you tell them to open their eyes. There will usually be general surprise and amusement when they see their positions and discover who it is they've been touching.

It is a good idea to try a similar exercise in pairs, telling each partner to feel and try to remember the texture and shape of the other's hands (rings are first removed). They then shut their eyes and you lead each person to another part of the room, well away from his partner. When everyone is re-positioned, ask them to go down to all fours and move like this around the room until they find their partners; they must, however, touch only the hands of anyone they meet during their search for the right partner. Once most of them have found their partners, suggest that they open their eyes and wait quietly for the rest to finish.

Variation   The group sit in a circle. Two chairs are put in the centre, side by side but with the seats facing in opposite directions. One person volunteers to sit in the centre, with eyes closed. A second person volunteers silently to be the 'victim' and sits in the other chair with eyes open. The first person must guess who the other is by touching only his head and face. A similar variation is to have one 'blind' person in the centre, who must first feel and memorise carefully the hands of one of the group and then try to identify them when confronted with the hands of the whole group.

Extension   In pairs. A is told that B is blind. B wishes to be taken out (to do some Christmas shopping, walk in the park in springtime, or some similar outing). A goes to Bs home and prepares him or her for the outing, decides whether to travel by bus, rail, or even underground, and gently takes care of B throughout the expedition, at the same time giving B a vivid commentary about the sights and the people he imagines they would encounter. B listens and may ask relevant questions or make comments. Encourage fluent, imaginative verbal description (suggest for the visit a district which the group knows well). The descriptions are well worth recording if you have a portable tape-recorder. This exercise helps to promote sensitivity and mutual give-and-take.

Variation   In groups of three. A is the leader, B is blind, C lame or badly hurt. They must decide where they are, why they are there, and what they need to do to leave the place. Introduce three obstacles which they must overcome (e.g. a tunnel, a bog, a narrow ledge).

For a follow-up to these exercises, see Journeys, pages 38–9.

Movement

The stance and movement of the body often expresses a person's feelings and attitudes as much as the tone of his voice and his choice of words. I have found that movement is a form of expression which seems to come more naturally and innately to some people than to others. Many diffident movers need the opportunity to learn how to move. If they are encouraged, they discover that it is a form of physical expression which they thoroughly enjoy, giving them a new confidence in communicating with others.

As a young teacher I was very anxious about my ability to teach movement. The children in the school to which I was appointed had previously had an excellent dance-drama teacher, which in itself was inhibiting. I found it terrifying to have to teach a class of thirty or more children while also operating a record-player, a loudspeaker and at least one record. By the time I had struggled into the room with the equipment and plugged it all in, and then located the right groove on the record, the children were up the wall bars or diving under the curtains. (The room was one of those all-purpose halls which do for school plays, physical education and school lunches.) So I changed my tactics, and decided to experiment with other stimuli for movement; and I discovered drums, cymbals, home-made percussion, and all the sounds the human voice can make other than chatter.

The ideas in this section will, I hope, give an indication of the different ways of starting off and exploring movement. The pooling of the group's ideas with those of the teacher is important, and the teacher should bear in mind that an idea which works for one group might not necessarily work for another. Thus it follows that the second group may suggest and develop an idea which the first group had found totally antipathetic. The most difficult part for the teacher is to decide which ideas should be kept for sustained work and which should be gently put aside and forgotten about. Some of my happiest and most successful sessions have failed abysmally when used with an alternative group, because I have assessed the group badly. This has often arisen through forcing an approach rather than letting it arise spontaneously.

Movement developing from verbal suggestions

When suggesting ways of moving, remember to get contrasting changes of pace and encourage direct and indirect movement, as well as movement which focuses on large and small parts of the body. Encourage absorption by constant concentration on the focus of the exercise, and praise enthusiastically once you see achievement, however slight. Remember that praise is always very encouraging when people have achieved something even slightly beyond normal expectations.

Sequence 1

The group covers the width and length of the room walking at a normal pace, but on the change signal (which can be either verbal or a drum beat) they must alter direction as well as pace, and travel round the room in one of the following ways: using large strides, on tiptoe, walking backwards, sideways and so on, any way other than on two feet, pacing their own initials on the floor, painting their initials on the floor.

Sequence 2—Strange walks

Let the general focus be to cover the length and breadth of the room, or limit everyone to a territory (e.g. they may only travel from the spot they are standing on to a spot a few feet away). Then let them either walk on tiptoe, sides of feet, heels, with very flat feet, or in some other way, and let the speed vary, either fast or slow; or let them move holding their ankles with their hands, holding calves, holding knees, holding tips of toes, holding insteps, holding heels, say. Encourage people to alter their head and body positions so that they complement the movement which the arms, hands and legs have structured.

Extension Ask them to form groups of about four or five. Each group tries out the different walks, and then selects the one they are most interested in developing. Encourage the development of a sound to go with the walk, and any other characteristic which might materialise. As a follow-up, imagine a meeting between different groups of people who live in a strange, weird town, or in another world. Or the sequence might lead to bird and animal movement, and improvisations could develop accordingly.

Sequence 3—Tracing out and repeating a pattern

Start off by letting each person select a territory (e.g. between the spot he is standing on and a spot a few feet away). Each may move within this span, directly or indirectly. The aim is to trace out a pattern or sequence of movements which can be repeated accurately at one set speed or in contrasting speeds. Next each person finds a partner and they teach one another their sequence of movements, so that each pair has two sequences of movement which the partners can repeat accurately together. This exercise may again be repeated by a pair creating a sequence within a territory and teaching it to another pair, then reversing roles, and so on, till the size of the group is quite considerably increased, depending upon the sustainment standard of the class you are working with at the time.

Sequence 4

Moving on a spot in different areas, and in one area and at contrasting speeds. See Sequence 2, page 9.

Sequence 5—Relating unrelated actions

As this is a difficult exercise, use it only with a group who are responding well to improvisation and can cope with more advanced work. It is a particularly useful exercise for unblocking an imaginative group who have become a little stale and trite in their approach to ideas. It is worked in pairs: A makes a movement, not leaving the spot he stands upon, B makes a second movement, again not moving off his spot, A makes a third movement. The movements should be spontaneous, and not related to each other; you could ask both A and B to do their movements with eyes shut, and memorise the action, then open their eyes and repeat exactly the movements they made before. Encourage very simple movements, and those determined by either contrasting speeds or by using large and small parts of the body. Reverse roles so that B starts first. After having experimented once or twice, suggest that they now take a sequence of three spontaneous alternative movements and this time repeat them several times, until a silent dialogue of movement between the pair emerges. The outcome of this dialogue can then be polished, and perhaps used as the basis for further improvised movement.

Sequence 6—Strange creatures

In pairs: A leans against B and B must anchor his body accordingly, so that he can support the weight of A; A should attempt to lean against different areas of B's body. Reverse roles.

B should now try to support and carry A from one part of the room to another. They should support each other back to back, side to side, and find out in how many ways this can be done, with the As holding, supporting or balancing parts of their partner's body and vice versa. Select one of these combinations and, as in the 'strange walks', let the rest of the two bodies, faces and so on complement the shape and movement implied.

Extension   Let these weird creatures form part of a story for young children (e.g. *Where the Wild Things Are* by Maurice Sendak, or for older children one of the Norse stories about trolls). An outer-space or science fiction type of story might be used by adults.

Sequence 7—Questions which encourage variety and focus

Before beginning to move to drum/cymbal/music/poem, each member of the group should decide on a starting position. Are they going to start high, low, curled, stretched, or how?

Which part of the body will move first: hand, elbow, hip, foot? In which direction will it go: forward, round, in/out, up/down?

Is the movement direct or indirect?

What speed will be used—quick, slow?

Remember contrasts of movement are positive (e.g. strong/light, curl/uncurl, contract/release, slow/sudden, straight/twist, angular/curving, etc.). Suggest that the group respond to the rhythm of a drum beat, and at the end of a sequence ask them to freeze into a particular shape (e.g. round, straight, wide, narrow, spiky, jagged, etc.).

With young children, get them to twist their bodies into the shapes of different letters of the alphabet. Then, as an extension, let each child represent one or two letters, and when you call out a word the children representing the letters in that word come out in turn and stand in a space to form the word. The letters may be flat or upright depending upon the children. This is a very amusing game, and can be developed to include commas, full stops, etc. Particularly successful if you have two teams competing against each other.

Sequence 8—Words as stimulus

The most suitable words are of course onomatopoeic, and to start with it is well worth sorting out for yourself a list of contrasting words. I have often used this exercise when working with a group who were good at movement but unimaginative vocally. We usually start by uttering various contrasting vocal sounds, first consonants, then vowels, for instance: t-t-t, t-t-t, t-t-t, ta, and then d-d-d, d-d-d, d-d-d-da, letting the weight and texture of the sound suggest a movement. Other pairs of consonants would be f/b, k/g, ch/j. Encourage the group to respond to the sound with the whole body as the sound is said. Suggest they utter the sound in different ways—loudly/quietly, happily/angrily, and so on. See that the body responds to the sound. Exciting visual and sound patterns can emerge from this work, particularly if a group find it amusing and interesting to experiment with.

After this suggest a word, for instance 'lightly'. You must now experiment with the word, and say it in a variety of ways—slowly, trippingly, with a pause between the syllables. Let the group respond to the sound that you give to the word. Choose another word (e.g. 'heavily'), and experiment with the way you say this word, letting the sounds you use be in contrast to the first word. The group might now form into pairs and work on words of their own choosing, responding to each other alternately by using contrasting words, which should be spoken and moved to simultaneously.

Once they have established the necessary understanding and are experimenting quite freely and happily with words and their sound qualities, and moving in response, then ask the group for an idea to which you could all contribute. For example, in order to create the quality of 'rain', consider together all the different types of rain that you have experienced, the way it flows off various surfaces, the effect it has on people, the relief and the sadness it can bring, and other qualities.

Each person then takes one word he associates with rain and to which he feels ready to respond in movement. The movement does not have to be a 'mime' of the word, merely a response to the word.

It is now time to experiment together. You may wish to put the words in a particular order; some could be repeated; they could all be said in a whisper, the third time loudly ('plop—plop—PLOP'), with the body responding to the light, light, HEAVY rhythm. It is difficult to give explicit instructions on how to create a word/movement poem, because it usually arises quite miraculously from a group whose imaginative chemistry just seems to fuse during a particular session. I have sometimes felt able to tell a group exactly how to achieve a word poem, but this always happens after they have successfully reached an exciting end-product, and as soon as I meet the succeeding group, the method I am advocating seems too muddled, too vague, and a glazed look of disbelief passes over their faces. The only thing to do is to start in the way I have suggested, and gradually build as the group gains confidence and dexterity with the idea.

Extension   Take a nursery rhyme that everyone in the group knows, and divide a large group into sets of about four to six. Let them experiment with the word sounds, the rhythms, juxtapose the lines and words and the order of the plot. Try adding a jazz rhythm, or work on it in slow motion, and see what the outcome is.

Touch exercise—finding your partner's hands

Hand exercises—as an individual

Sequence 9—Conversations with different parts of the body

The first exercise involves only the arms and hands, with the focus on the hands and fingers. Let everyone work on his own. The aim is to encourage the creation of a conflict or a feeling of sympathy between the right and left hands. For instance, you might suggest that (*a*) the right is subordinate to the left, which is very dominant; (*b*) the left has great difficulty in moving, whereas the right moves freely and fast; (*c*) they both want to meet but there is a force keeping them from touching; and so on. I find it helps to demonstrate this exercise.

You might also like to try working in pairs, and letting an unspoken dialogue occur between the four hands. If the group seems interested, extend this further by suggesting they initiate conversations between elbows, shoulders, feet, noses, and so on.
Extension Suitable for groups of four to six. The groups should kneel in a circle with hands on the ground, facing in towards the centre of the circle. The wrists should remain on or close to the floor.

Hand exercises—as a group

The aim is to discover how the various fingers and hands react to each other spontaneously. You may find that some groups need the opportunity to experiment with this exercise several times (not always in the same session) in order to alleviate aggressive instincts. The exercise can promote sensitivity and absorption, and give rise to terrific moments of suspense.

Extension Passing messages non-verbally, in pairs. A has to decide what B is looking at (the object may be imaginary) and vice versa. Once the pairs seem to be working reasonably happily, develop the exercise. A tells B what to do merely by using the eyes, forehead and nose (he must not mime words with his mouth). It will occur to you while you are working that there are a number of ways of extending this exercise. For instance, A could decide on a particular mood and the reason for it and try to project this mood to B.

Sequence 10—Proverbs expressed in action

Quite a lighthearted, fun exercise. Individually, in pairs, or better still in small groups of four or five, everyone has to mime a proverb which you either tell them or write down on a card. Other groups can guess what the proverb is, or it can be a competition against time won by the quickest group to mime the proverb clearly and with wit.

Sequence 11—Stage fights

Invaluable if you have a group of restless boys or moody girls; and all groups should learn the techniques required for delivering a bloody punch or a killing kick. The main moves in stage fights are the slap, the punch, hair-pulling, kicking, nose and ear pulling, the faint. These moves are very difficult to describe briefly. An excellent book has been written on stage fights (by W. Hobbs; see book list, page 137) and I would suggest you read it and perhaps find an amateur actor who would be happy to teach you 'the tricks of the trade'. They are very easy to learn, and are based on the idea that you do not hurt the other person. If you touch him, it must be gently, most of the anguish is shown by the victim, who can squeal and screech to his heart's content. I once had a group of very moody teenage girls who thought drama was 'stupid', so we used to have discussions about their problems. One day a fight was brewing in the group, and I suggested that the girl who was spoiling for a good blood-and-thunder outside the school gates should take me on. I taught them the rules and the main moves, and then asked this girl to be my partner and demonstrate the moves. I was the victim the first time and demonstrated with vigour, as she very gently twisted me round by the tip of my nose and punched me, without hurting, in the stomach. On the next round she was delighted to be victim, I think she had found the role of aggressor a little too much with a screaming, writhing teacher egging her on. She demonstrated superbly, the class sat with eyes on stalks. A few minutes afterwards, when everyone was in full combat, the Deputy Head arrived: the classroom was overlooked by an apartment block; and the residents had been watching the awful proceedings and had come round to complain. I was advised to use a more secluded room for stage fights in future!

Movement developing from vocal sounds

Sequence 1—Slow and quick movements stimulated by appropriate sounds

See Sequence 3, pages 10–11. Encourage sounds which are really slow or really quick, and let people make low sounds in the floor area and high ones in the head area.

Sequence 2—Teaching a partner a sound and movement

There should be quite a considerable gap between A and B—at least nine to twelve feet. A makes a very simple movement and accompanying sound and approaches B. A then teaches B the movement and sound, and B gradually leaves the spot he has been standing on and moves off with A's sound and movement. A stops moving. B moves to a space away from A, and gradually changes the original movement and sound. The change should merely be an adaptation of the original, not a sudden alteration. Once B is happy with the adaptation, he takes it back to A and teaches A the new movement and sound. A then moves away and adapts this pattern to another pattern, and returns to B.

Encourage simple movements, and the flowing of one sound and movement pattern into another.

Variation   This exercise can involve the whole group. People scatter themselves in a space round the room. One person starts, and teaches his pattern to a second, who takes it into a space and adapts it; once familiar with the adaptation, he goes to a third person and teaches that person the new movement, sound pattern and so on.

Encourage the group to experiment with the different body levels and make the sounds appropriate to the movements.

Extension   Experiment yourself, by letting the As make a sound suitable for the Bs to move to (e.g. A^1 makes a sound, B^1 moves to the sound, then A^2 makes the accompanying sound for B^2 and so on). Sometimes all the As make a group sound to which all the Bs move simultaneously. Roles can then be reversed. If you and the group are interested in this type of sound and movement you will develop numerous permutations on a theme.

Sequence 3—Piece of magic yarn

I developed this exercise from an operation I had had on my gum after which, for several days, a long black stitch hung over my front teeth. The children I was teaching were fascinated by this black string in my mouth, so I suggested that in some of the crannies between the floor tiles there were some little bits of yarn (imagined, of course). I demonstrated by digging down one little furrow with the tip of my nail; nothing happened. 'You see,' I said, 'you have to look very carefully.' I then felt between another couple of tiles and, lo and behold, my nail brought up a little bit of yarn. 'Listen, it makes a sound!' The class could then hear a tiny, faint sound. The sound got stronger as the piece of yarn grew. I showed how it could change shape, and how it could be used in a variety of ways. 'However, if you let go of it, it jumps back into its little cave.' This exercise caused a lot of fun, even after my black stitch had been removed. It is a good opening exercise with responsive adults, and can lead to many variations. With younger children it is a good start for the story of *Jack and the Beanstalk*.

Sequence 4—Growing with a sound

The group scatters and everyone finds a space on his own. Everyone should let himself shrink into a very small curled-up shape on the floor. Once there is an atmosphere of over-all stillness, suggest that all begin to hear a very, very tiny sound coming from the floor. To start with the body moves very slightly to this sound, but as the sound gets stronger, the body grows according to the type of sound which is evolving. Once the sound and movement have reached full capacity, suggest that people work together—perhaps they move round till a similar sound is found, or opposite sounds might work together.

Encourage absolute stillness at the beginning of the exercise, with a very tiny, slight sound and very minute movement to start with and then rhythmic sound and movement. It often helps if you can darken the room you are working in, or light it rather patchily.

Extension Experiment with this exercise; one interesting thing to do is to let the group huddle together, very small, and crouched in the centre of the space. They all make an extremely light, tiny sound, just a hum, or burr, which gradually develops; at the same time their bodies begin to stir to this faint sound and there is a rustle of movement. As the sound develops, the body movements grow, and the group gradually breaks up as individual movements and sounds emerge from the throng. I sometimes suggest that the evolving sound and movement should become quite rhythmic, and eventually everyone discovers a rhythmic movement and a rhythmic sound. This might suggest a theme—birth to death, or the growth of civilisation. You will find that as you watch, and encourage the group to talk about their work, ideas for taking the exercises further will emerge and a different approach will often be apparent with successive groups.

See also Greetings (pages 36–7); Numbered and lettered groups (pages 39–40)

Movement developing from percussion

Sequence 1

Listen to sounds and discuss what they could represent. See
Sequence 1, page 8.

Sequence 2—Letting one sound develop into an improvisation

I usually find the cymbal the most effective instrument to start with,
as the sounds it produces are quite evocative. The group should
listen to the sound first, either standing up in a space or sitting on
the floor, with eyes shut; it often works well if they are standing up,
ready for action. People then say what the sound makes them think
of. Take one of these ideas, preferably one which has been
suggested by several people, and begin to develop an improvisation
in mime and movement, with the one sound as stimulus. One group
I was working with felt that the cymbal sound I was tapping represented a bell in a Spanish church—the day was very hot and the
people were slowly getting themselves ready for a funeral. The dead
man was an important official in the town. Slowly a procession
formed, while others became elderly onlookers. The procession
moved towards the church door, but one old lady remained weep-
ing outside. She was apparently the excommunicated daughter of
the dead man.

Sequence 3—Five limb movements and one body movement

This exercise has been a great help when I have wanted a group to
work in a very stylised way. You need a drum or a resonant tin
wastepaper bin. Bang the drum five times quite slowly and rhythmi-
cally: on each beat everyone moves his head in one direction and
holds it there till the next beat, while his body remains absolutely
still. However on the sixth beat, which should be stressed firmly, the
body adopts a different position. The position must be secure, so
that it can be held rigidly. Then the rhythm is repeated again, but
this time with four head movements and on the fifth stressed beat, a
body movement. You may carry on to three head movements, then

two, then one. This may be reversed. Encourage focused movement and strong body changes. Experiment by letting the group work with other parts of the body (an arm, a hand, say) on the small beats. When the group have become proficient, let them divide into small groups and work on a sequence based on the rhythm previously explored.

Sequence 4—Making musical instruments

Plan this session in advance. Ask the group to make and bring with them a home-made instrument which will make a sound without too much effort, and which is easily portable. Instruments can be made from boxes filled with split peas, large sheets of crackly paper, rubber bands stretched round a box, cooking tins, bottles which can be blown against, for instance. It is helpful to establish a rule that when the instruments are not being used they are placed on the floor, and are neither touched, rolled, nor shaken. Otherwise, with a large group, there is bedlam.

For the first part of the exercise, aim to get everyone standing in a space, and suggest that they find a good starting position, holding their instruments. Each should then move according to the sound of his instrument. The sound of the instrument and the way in which it is handled causes the body to move in a particular way. If people are inhibited, let them roll, shake or swing the instruments, but at the same time let the body follow the movement and react to the sound. Once the group seems fairly at ease, suggest that the different instruments are exchanged, so that everyone has to adapt his movements to a new sound and a new shape.

Extension In pairs, A and B. Encourage a good starting position, with each partner holding his own instrument. The aim of the exercise is to make a conversation between the instruments and the 'attached' bodies. A moves towards B (or he might wish to circle round B or to hover away from B); B replies and A listens, standing still or holding the position he stopped at. Then A responds to B's sound, and so on. Encourage them to develop a positive dialogue—one might turn out to be more dominant than the other; they might both be conspiring or gossiping together; or they might explore one sound by repeating it with both instruments. For instance A makes a sound, B repeats the sound and movement but changes it and gives A the changed sound and movement, which A repeats and then alters accordingly. Encourage the sounds to play off one another, so that there is variety and precision of movement.

Sequence 5—Atmosphere from sounds

Let the different instruments group themselves together, and suggest that each group works on a piece of sound music—which can either be used 'live' or can be taped and explored on the tape recorder at different speeds.

Music as a stimulus for movement

The method I have found most acceptable is described in Chapter 3 in the section on Stories from sounds and music, pages 70–1.

Poetry and song as a stimulus for movement

If a group has been responsive to the exercise using words as a stimulus for movement (pages 25–6), you will probably find that they will enjoy moving to a poem. Look for alliterative poems, and those using onomatopoeic words; they do not have to tell a story or be realistic, but should be evocative, melodic, or rhythmic. For instance, I have used some of T. S. Eliot's 'The Rock' part VII, and the choruses from Greek plays. There have been one or two anthologies compiled of poems suitable for movement and dance (see book list, pages 136–7).

Ballads and folksongs are an excellent basis for work. I had one group of rather lethargic teenage girls who finally moved quite sensitively to Joan Baez's 'Mary Hamilton'. They had rejected most of the other work I had tried to encourage them to do, but enjoyed discussions arising from some of the Beatles' songs and showed more awareness than I had expected from listening to Bob Dylan and Julie Felix.

Many groups have written and composed music to create their own songs, and then choreographed movement to complement the songs. I have no knowledge of music and can play no instrument and so have given them very little assistance. There have usually been one or two people in the group with a good ear; we have never used a piano or a guitar. Words would be written, usually in the form of a poem, although sometimes in definite song form. The people who could compose a tune would take the words away and play around with them. When they returned they either recorded the songs on tape so that the rest of the group could listen to the recording, or they sang the words and tune to the group who picked them up accordingly. The tape recorder was an invaluable asset, as it was the only way we could notate our tune. Some groups were very diffident about making up a tune, and then I suggested they took a familiar tune—from a nursery rhyme or folk song—and adapted the words and tune accordingly. I've found this works very well with young children.

Developing abstract interpretations of a theme

Some groups will be quite prepared to take an idea and explore it in its abstract or symbolic form. This is often exciting, and gives a group confidence in the depth of their imagination, as it is a very fulfilling way of experimenting together. After working through improvisations on a number of ideas, insight can get a little dulled, and to explore conventional, realistic situations in another way sharpens the wits. The outcome can be exhilarating.

The exercises in this section are devised to encourage the emergence of fresh and spontaneous ideas; most of them need the preliminary concentration and movement exercises already described.

Sequence 1—Numbered and lettered groups and people

The group should divide into small sets of four or five. Each set should have a number, and each person within the set a letter. If you call out 'Ds', all the Ds lead their own sets, but if you call 'D⁴', then only D in set 4 is responsible for the antics of the whole class. This exercise is similar to teaching a partner a movement and sound (Sequence 2, page 30). The person who starts teaches the group or set a very simple movement and accompanying sound, and the others must follow the leader as precisely as possible. The leader must keep the movement very simple and successive leaders (called for by the teacher) should aim to alter the speed and the area of their movement, so that the group experiences quite a constrast of patterns. If possible, encourage the sets to carry on with the first movement until the second leader has worked out something suitable, so that you avoid a sort of limbo stage when everyone stands around waiting for a new structure or pattern to be adapted from the previous one. When all the sets are following one group leader, again try to avoid a limbo phase by telling them to carry on with their pattern till D⁴ has communicated the over-all pattern to his own set. To break them up into sets again you merely call out another letter, and the people with that letter adapt D⁴'s pattern to something else.

This is a lovely exercise for group co-ordination. I have also found it excellent for themes connected with chaos, for instance the beginning of the world; or a situation connected with commuters going to work arriving and settling into their day-to-day grooves. Again encourage the class to give you their ideas and interpretations.

Sequence 2—Greetings

This is a marvellous exercise which evolved originally with a group of twelve-year-olds. It encourages timing, punctual cueing, unblocking of the imagination, and uninhibited movements and sounds. You may use either the body and vocal sounds, or the body and home-made instruments.

The group stands in a large circle, with plenty of space in the centre for action. The aim is for people to move into the centre in turn, each making a sound and a complementary movement which he must keep to until the conclusion of the sequence. The first person advances to the centre and then freezes, the second person comes in and, on reaching the centre, is greeted by the first person using the movement and sound he has invented. The second person greets in reply. They are joined by a third person, and the ritual pattern of greeting is repeated. It is important to keep to the order of greeting when first playing the game; the players do not have to remain stationary when they greet or are greeted by a new entrant. Gradually, as more people come into the circle, an interesting pattern of sounds and movements emerges from the various reactions to the 'greetings'.

After one or two exploratory attempts, encourage the group to adapt the rules as reactions spontaneously trigger off other variations. Encourage a variety of people to make the first move into the circle, for the natural leader should not always feel that he must make the first move. If there is a long gap before the first player enters, or between players entering, suggest that they 'break', as the atmosphere will have gone cold and it will be too difficult for players to enter spontaneously. Or, if the group is slow to move, let the centre players invite others from the circle into the gathering. Also encourage the use of plenty of contrasting sounds and variations of sound level and speed of movement, so that the patterns in the centre appear to be an ever-changing kaleidoscope of sound and movement. Be ready to 'break' the action as soon as you are aware of its becoming soggy or repetitive or beginning to disintegrate.

When the exercise is working smoothly, suggest a freeze in the centre and ask the watching players to consider what the frozen group might represent. From their various suggestions, select one and let the players in the centre bring the scene realistically to life using words. The character each adopts should be related vocally and physically to his original sound and movements.

Follow this up by trying the same formula using home-made percussion instruments, and masks.

Sequence 3—String

Acquire a large ball of fairly thick string (or tie together old nylon stockings so that you have a very long nylon rope) and make a circle by tying the two ends together. One person takes hold of part of the string, the next takes another section. The string must be held taut between the two. Players continue to pick up sections of the string,

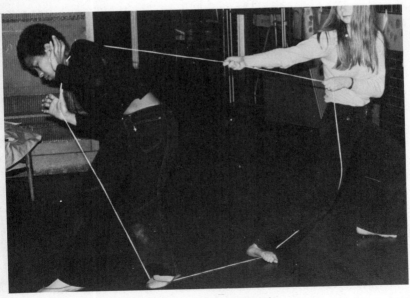

String exercise—as a pair

keeping it taut all the time, until the string is used up and is being held very taut by everyone. All may then slowly move, section by section, varying the shape made by the string according to their own positions—the shape will, of course, alter as people move across the floor, on to higher areas (rostra or chairs) or lie or kneel on the floor. It may be fun to let any extra players crawl through the string. This is particularly enjoyed when younger children are invited to join in, and the huge spider web construction could easily become the focus of a scene in an improvised play for young children.

Variation   With shorter lengths of string you can let the group form small sets of two or three, experimenting with the string in as many ways as possible. You could get the group to make an interesting mobile set from this simple device.

Sequence 4—Journeys

The group should previously have had some experience of the blind/trust exercises already mentioned (page 19). One person volunteers to be the traveller. Warn him that it will be necessary for him to keep his eyes shut throughout the journey; although the experience will be strange, he must trust the group implicitly. The group members are warned that they will have failed if they hurt or destroy the trust of the traveller. They must watch the traveller all the time, and never take him beyond the limits of his trust. The traveller goes outside the room and awaits his journey. The group plan the journey. They may decide on any situation or any place; I have known groups to create a funfair, an accident, a farm, a day in the country including a boat trip, an adventure in space, a tunnel of horrors, a coronation. They create the sequence by using their own bodies, vocal sounds, and any pieces of material which happen to be in the room. The journey must start from the moment the traveller, with eyes shut, enters the room. Words need not be spoken unless they are to reassure the traveller. If he has to be picked up (as in an accident) it must be with enormous care and consideration.

It is often wise to let the 'journey' be the culmination of sessions working on trust and blind movement. An enjoyable extension of some of the partner work which leads into journeys is to follow the partner by his sound. A leads and B follows with eyes shut; A makes the sound he is going to use as B's guide, and B follows the direction of this sound. A needs cunningly to manipulate the direction so that sometimes the sound is on a high level, sometimes on a low level, and so on. Another worthwhile experience which can be enjoyed in a journey exercise is cradling. You need a minimum of three people to make up a group, the centre person shuts his eyes and gently falls forwards, backwards or sideways against the other two, who support his weight. If a gentle humming or chant is added, you can create a delicious sensation of peace and trust. (The person in the centre should fall from a balanced position: the body should remain quite straight and the feet, firmly placed on the ground, act as a pivot.)

Not every group is capable of the responsibility of constructing a journey; the group needs to be sensitive, imaginative and co-operative.

Extension If the group has enjoyed working out journeys involving body and sound, set them the task of creating an environment made from different types of waste paper, wrapping, boxes, and so on. They can add lights and/or tape-recordings of sounds, and either use it for their own enjoyment or arrange for some visitors to participate.

Sequence 5—Groups at a party

Suitable for adults or imaginative teenagers. Groups of four to six are formed. They stand in a circle. One person is spare, and as he moves up to a group, someone else leaves that group and fits into another group, and so on. Within each group there is quite a complicated pattern of communication. One person talks at a time but only the odd word is uttered out loud, the rest of the sentence is a mutter, logical but inarticulate, about his associations with the audible word. Anyone who is stuck for something to say can latch on to ideas associated with someone else's audible word.

Sequence 6—Speaking in numbers or letters and in gibberish

Each person in the group tries to introduce himself to as many other people as possible while you are counting slowly to a given figure such as twenty-five. However, they may only speak to each other in numbers. It is helpful to limit the numbers, using, say, only those between 1 and 10. Encourage people to use as wide a range of vocal tone, emphasis and inflection as possible, to indicate the attitude and mood of the person they are portraying. The numbers may be spoken in any order, using as few or as many as desired within the agreed range.

You might like to give the group characters in a particular situation, such as a large convention of sales representatives for different
goods. Try a 'greetings' exercise with the group, adapting it as you
go along. (See Sequence 2 of this section, pages 36–7.) Or suggest
that they work in pairs, A and B. A has invented a new product and
is trying to convince a manufacturer, B, of its worth. B is secretly
interested in the product but needs to be convinced that it is a good
selling investment. These exercises could also be done using letters
instead of numbers.

Instead of using a number or letter language, a language can be
made up of sounds. Work in pairs with A as the master, B the pupil.
A teaches B a sound, which B repeats and thus learns. In this way A
goes on to teach B a new language. You may suggest that A teaches B
three simple one-syllable sounds, and two or three two-syllable
sounds, and then they join up these sounds to make phrases which
can be understood by their tone, emphasis, pitch and stress. In fact,
they have invented a language which both can understand. A then
proceeds to teach B an occupation. He must not use any words, the
explanation must be completely in gibberish. Once B is proficient at
doing the occupation, you could suggest that the pairs might like to
demonstrate their occupations to the rest of the group. Questions in
gibberish should be encouraged.

The development may tend to go in many ways. I have found this
a useful exercise for all voice work, and for helping people to understand that it is not what they say, but how they say it, that matters.
Improvised plays based on ideas such as the conquest of the Incas,
the arrival of man on an inhabited planet in space, and even Lewis
Carroll's 'Jabberwocky' have grown from gibberish.

Developing a character, or becoming someone else

As you will have discovered in the movement exercises, some
people can instinctively portray different characters, the majority
can make a good attempt at playing a stock-character type in an
improvisation, and there are many who tend, at first, to play themselves when improvising. Therefore, we need to devise exercises
which are particularly concerned with character development. You
must be prepared for the fact that a certain number in any group will
rely solely on stock characterisation in their improvisations.

Younger children usually play themselves or very broad stock types. With a teenage or adult group it helps to have some discussion about people. I encourage classes to take an interest in the way people move, use mannerisms, dress, react to situations, reminding them that to stare point-blank at a stranger is not the most tactful way to study the human ape. If they are regularly encouraged to be aware of people in the street and elsewhere, their perception deepens, and if the exercises are based on this kind of research and observation, then the characters that are assumed tend to be 'real' rather than cartoons.

Sequence 1—Personification of objects

This is excellent for young children, although it can be used with an adult group if the members are responsive. Everyone should find himself a space on the floor and make himself into the shape you suggest (e.g. round, long and thin, wide and square, jagged, spiky, oval). Ask them all to make themselves quite comfortable in the shape you have asked for and then think of an object which is shaped in the same way; they are not to tell you what the object is till the exercise is over. I find it helps if everyone has his eyes shut, as there is a lot of imagining to do. Give people a little time to think about the object they are representing; if they are very young children you might give them a few ideas, for instance: 'Are you really round? What object is really round? You must be careful to think of an object—something which does not move, or grow, or breathe. Perhaps you might be a round red apple in a bowl, or you might be an old rubber ball. Think very hard. I'm soon going to ask you some questions, which you will listen to and then answer but without speaking, just imagining you are part of the answer. Remember no one is to call out, there will be a chance to tell me what you are when you have finished imagining all the answers.'

For a teenage or adult group, your questions might include some of the following:

What colour are you, are you the same colour all over?

Are you a hard object or a soft object?

Are you old or are you new?

Might you be owned by anyone? Does your owner treat you well?—Or perhaps you haven't got an owner?

Where are you positioned? Do you like being where you are?

What other objects can you see from the position you have

Object simulation—a boulder

imagined yourself to be in? Can you perhaps see live things, things which breathe, grow and move?

How could you move? Have you ever been moved? Perhaps the wind would help you to change position, or it might be a hand, or a foot.

Look, you are about to be moved. How is it happening? Let me see you move. Where have you been put?

I have suggested rather a lot of questions; you will need to judge the number the group can cope with. Also you will need to allow for pauses, so that everyone has ample opportunity for working out an answer.

Several experiments with this exercise should prove worth while. Suggest each time that the members of the group assume a different shape. Once you feel confident that they are thinking out their own answers quite happily, you can just ask them to think of an object which sits on the window sill, or on top of a shelf, or on a table.

Object simulation—a sewing machine

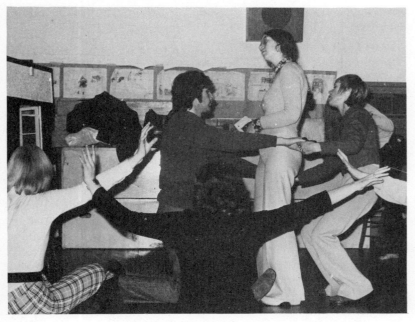

Object simulation—a boat

Object simulation—emerging from the ruins

Responsive groups can take the exercise further in any of the following ways:

1 Working with partners, A models B into an object and tells B that he is, for instance, a pincushion, then what colour it is, if the pincushion is old or new, and so on.
2 (This is not very appropriate for young children.) Each pair selects two objects and improvises spontaneously a scene involving these two objects. Remind them that their voices must suit the type and age of the object concerned.
3 By now you could suggest a situation which might involve the whole group. Children often suggest ideas as a toyshop, goods for sale in a shop window, or a puppet master and his puppets. Ask your group for suggestions and develop the idea. Ideas might come from stories and poems, such as *Coppelia*, *The Borrowers* by Mary Norton, 'The Broom, the Shovel, the Poker and the Tongs' by Edward Lear. With older children (12 upwards) let them consider more bizarre situations, where you might have objects conniving with each other about the human beings in whose midst they live (e.g. goods in a sale room, ornamental garden objects, the cutlery on a dining table). Ways of working with a story are explained in Chapter 3.

Sequence 2—Animals, birds and insects

One of the finest descriptions of encouraging children to imagine themselves to be an animal is written in Rose Bruford's *Teaching Mime* (see book list, page 136). I have found her method quite foolproof with a reasonably responsive group. This sort of work can only be achieved with an imaginative and courageous group of adults or children. If you are unable to find *Teaching Mime*, then I suggest you use the ideas given in Sequence 1 above, asking the group to become animals instead of objects. Situations involving animals might include: trapped in a cage; spider and fly; mouse and cat; escape from a zoo; preparing for hibernation; pets in a household; stray animals.

Stories to work from could include *The Wind in the Willows*, *The Hundred and One Dalmatians*, the works of Beatrix Potter, Aesop's Fables, Noah, *Chanticleer and the Fox*.

Sequence 3—Statues or waxworks

I find this works best if I get the group moving to a strong, slow beat (on a drum, for instance)—one, two, three, four, *five*—on the fifth beat you call out the name of a famous character, a type of person, or an animal. For example, with everyone moving to the beat, you call out, 'A bad-tempered colonel'. Everyone freezes instantly into the character. On the next set of beats they must move as the bad-tempered colonel, but when the next character is called they transform themselves into a dragon, a national hero, Humpty Dumpty, or whatever it may be.

Sequence 4—Pulling faces

The group sit on the floor in pairs, facing each other. Start by getting them to massage their own faces gently, and while doing this to become aware of the many different surfaces. I prefer them to do this with their eyes shut. If they are very responsive and sensitive, you might like to have them massaging each other's faces very deftly.

Give them some ideas for flexing various parts of their faces—e.g. nose, eyes, forehead screwed up, then the whole face relaxed so that the jaw flops open like a goldfish—discovering how many parts of the face can be stretched just by using the facial muscles. Then get

Aggression

them to pull as many different types of face as possible—ugly, stern, curious, frightened, joyful, and so on.

Still in pairs, they then begin to develop the exercise together. A pulls an ugly face, then B has to make a carbon copy of it; reverse roles and ask B to make an equally unfortunate face. After a while warn the group you are going to ask them to freeze the face they have made. Then tell them that they are two people who are in conversation with each other, and without altering the expression they are wearing they should continue with the conversation. If they are not very spontaneous, give them a little more on which to base their conversations, by asking them questions—Are they relatives? Where have they met before? Where are they now?

Extension   The group should now be ready to stand up and find movements and mannerisms to suit some of their facial expressions. If they are responding well, let them find new partners for yet another conversation.

Variation—Throwing faces   The group sit in a circle and, as a beginning, you suggest a frowning face. Someone volunteers to start off. He establishes a frowning face and then, as if it were a mask, he takes it off and throws it towards someone else, who immediately assumes a frown. This person then pulls it off and throws it to someone else, and so on. To complicate the game, another person can volunteer to wear a smiling face, which is also pulled off and thrown at someone else and so on. You now have a frown and a smile being thrown round the circle. Some people land up with both frown and smile and have speedily to wipe one off and throw it away before assuming the other. Again, as the group become more proficient, they will be able to adopt more subtle expressions to throw to one another.

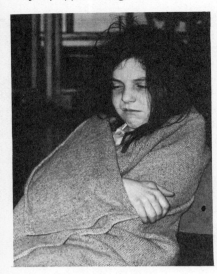

A tramp

Sequence 5—Creating a character to fit a picture

A good selection of pictures and photos of different types of people is a useful resource in developing a character from observation. Collect them from magazines and newspapers, and suggest that members of the group make their own collections. A useful way to start is to let the group divide into pairs (or threes) and give each pair one picture of a person between them. In turn, the pairs create a character and a life-history to fit the person in the picture. If the picture is in black-and-white, they will have to give details such as the person's colouring and so on. Try not to allow one person to add all the details; it is worthwhile suggesting that each adds one characteristic at a time in rotation. When they have made up a life-history as well as a character assessment of the person in the picture, they can then try 'being' that person. At this stage there are several ways of helping them to create an identifiable character:

1 Divide the pairs or threes so that partners are mixed up, but with each individual maintaining the character he has been preparing within his original group, so that two or three characters will now meet. If you prefer, they can give a brief description of themselves and thus work out a situation which is dependent on their knowing each other. The action should be based on a situation rather than just a meeting between two strangers.

2 Two sub-groups join together so that you have either six or four
   people. If there are two groups of three, the two As are the
   characters, the two Bs are the voices, and the two Cs are the
   conscience (unspoken thoughts of the character). A situation is
   devised accordingly. Reverse the roles, so that each person within
   the group has an opportunity to play the other roles, and after
   each exploration, let the individual groups discuss the 'truthful-
   ness' of the character. Is it identifiable? How far has it developed
   from the original conception? Is it yet another cartoon variation of
   a real person?

For pairs you need slightly different instructions. The two As are the
character and they can speak but have no control over the action or
the situation. The two Bs are the narrators and they tell the characters what to do, while developing a story between themselves. At
times they may indicate that the characters can speak; for instance:

NARRATOR B^1: As Fred reached forward to open the latch, Tim said
     cautiously—
CHARACTER A^1 (TIM): Fred, I don't know whether I should come in
     . . . it's rather late.
NARRATOR B^2 *(carrying on the narrative):*
     The gate was open, Fred shoved Tim through without cere-
     mony, and Tim thought to himself—

Character A^2 then speaks Tim's thoughts as if to an imaginary audience, and the narration is continued when Tim has finished speaking.

Sequence 6—Playing characters as animals or birds

A useful exercise for a group whose members find it hard to progress
from being themselves to being someone else. You can use the
pictures again, or you can write out on cards brief descriptions, or
even simply the names of various specific occupations. The cards are
distributed one to each person, and everyone must then quickly
assume the occupation described on his card. A second card, bearing the name of an animal, bird or insect, is picked by each player
who must now move and speak in the manner of the creature
chosen but also in character with the occupation on the first card. As
an example, the cards might be 'a traffic warden' and 'a sparrow'.
   The object is to encourage each person to work out the
mannerisms, both vocal and physical, that go with his character;
thus, in the above example, the traffic warden would probably move

and speak in a rather twittery and birdlike way. Small groups of three or four members are formed, and the players in each group tell each other their occupations but not their creatures. Each group then decides on an imagined place where the characters will meet— for example, in a bus shelter on a wet day. Spontaneous improvisations should be encouraged without any more time for discussion. It is useful to follow up the improvised activity with a discussion in which the players talk about how they went about giving their characters attitudes and movements different from their own and derived from the creatures on their cards. If you wish, the people in each group can guess each other's creatures, but this tends to lead to a rather superficial, exaggerated form of 'acting', when the object is to build up an inner thought process.

Sequence 7—Exaggerated movements leading to characterisation

Suitable for a group of teenagers or adults; if carefully organised this is excellent for a moody, lethargic group.

Everyone should be spaced out equidistantly around the room. They are to move on a firm, solid beat of one—two—three—four, but may only walk across the room in straight lines; the movement must be very formal and military, with eyes focused on a point straight ahead. However, if they wish to change direction, they must make a precise, neat, right-angled turn. I find it helps to demonstrate this movement; the right-angled turn needs a little practice, particularly if the floor is slippery. Allow a fair amount of practice time. Some groups enjoy getting used to the symmetry of the movement, and some excel at making the exercise really crisp and precise.

If two people meet coming from opposite directions, they should both stop and greet each other. The greeting should be brief. You might suggest that they acknowledge each other by a gesture, or by a gesture and a sound, then progress to one word, and so on. When they part, they must again make a precise right-angled turn.

You can now begin to build a character from movement. Continuing with the right-angled direct movement, ask everyone to protrude one part of his body only. For the first run-through suggest a part yourself (e.g. knees, nose, elbows). The protrusion should be very exaggerated, and in the first instance the focus should be totally on this one protrusion. Gradually the movement should develop to suggest a character who tends to walk with all the emphasis on this particular part of the body (there is no need for people to meet at this stage of the exercise). Again it may be helpful to ask various rhetorical questions about the assumed character: Where are you? Why are you there? Are you moving somewhere particular? What is your name? Your age? What do you do for a living? Why are you wearing those particular clothes? What do you like doing? What do you dislike doing? (I now suggest that they speak out their thoughts, very quietly.) Where were you born? Do you still see your parents? And so on. Once the majority seem quite absorbed in their characters, suggest that each character moves to a place which he or she likes. It should be apparent that the character enjoys doing something in this particular place. Then ask the character to move to another place, but this time without pleasure as the place is uncongenial; he must make it clear why he finds the place unpleasant.

Using a similar formula, let the group develop several different characters. When they seem ready you could suggest they use the meeting part of the exercise suggested above.

Sequence 8—Cross-examination

A useful extension to the previous exercise. A circle of chairs is made. The characters which have been established during the exercise in Sequence 7 are invited to sit down. One at a time they ask each other questions about themselves; both the questions and the answers should be in character. It sometimes works well if you put one chair a little on its own within the circle, and select one person to be the first candidate. In turn, the rest of the group question this person. Once the group is satisfied that they have learnt a little about the first character, a second volunteer is asked to sit in the chair.

Sequence 9—No two beings are exactly the same

This is an exercise to show that the differences between people are not so much related to occupation as to personal idiosyncrasies. Everyone in the group has the same occupation (e.g. cleaners, bus conductors, teachers). You decide during discussion the place in which the people would naturally meet during their work (e.g. teachers in a staff-room). Everyone then finds a space, and may use a chair or a stool. Tell them that the alarm clock is just about to ring, and they are to go through a morning's routine leading up to their arrival at the place of work. The situation then develops.

In the park

Although it is a little risky, it works much better if you resolve not to plot any further. I often take part as one of the group and help to ignite a situation through pertinent questioning. This exercise is particularly stimulating once you know and have confidence in your group; they will enjoy it if you take part as long as you are one of the team and don't take a star role!

Role-play

How role-play differs from improvised drama

The objectives of role-play are in no way concerned with perform-ance, acting, visual presentation, or any form of theatre. It is a method of working which helps individuals to be more fully aware of different attitudes, and the fact that there are various ways of solving a particular problem. The participants are asked to identify closely but objectively with another person, or with a situation, i.e. to consider what it is like to be in someone else's shoes, or to be confronted with a particular problem when the character is in a certain situation. They then seek various solutions to the problem and circumstances described by the leader. The participants concentrate on the attitude of the character, and there is no need for them to assume any physical or vocal mannerisms. The work does not require any form of audience as it is not concerned with the quality of the action, but the simulated experience should give deeper personal insight into any given problem and help to make a more relevant discussion. The participants should be encouraged to keep within the teacher's brief, and to re-enact the circumstances in their own way. The instructions may be verbal or written.

A simple way of conducting a role-play sequence might arise, for example, from group discussion on the problems facing sales representatives, and the group may decide that some practical exploration of the problem would help people to identify a little more closely with the argument. The group form pairs, A and B; A initially takes the role of customer while B is sales representative for, say, a particular type of electric typewriter, which he knows that A's firm is interested in installing for its secretarial staff. The As and the Bs are given separate private instructions, as this aids personal motivation. The instructions to the As, the customers, might be:

'You are trying to decide between B's firm and another reputable firm for the purchase of this particular electric typewriter. You must be totally convinced that you are making the right decision, as you are new to the job. You cannot afford to make a bad deal at this stage in your career.'

The instructions to the Bs, the sales representatives, might be:

'You have had an exceptionally bleak couple of months' business. Although you started off well, you cannot now acquire sufficient orders to make an adequate sales commission. If you were given this order it would help your profit balance.'

The teacher might then say to the whole group, 'How do two people with these problems interact? How does the encounter affect the individuals personally?' The teacher needs to emphasise that the outcome is not as significant as the thought processes which lead to the different individual reactions during the encounter.

The analytical discussion following a practical sequence is vital. It is the time when the group are given the opportunity to evaluate their feelings and ideas, for the discussion stems from the experiences in which they have actively participated or have just witnessed. The teacher should make every effort to encourage each person in the group to make an active contribution to the discussion. In some cases he will need to support those people who are not accustomed to talking freely within a group. A good teacher needs to be sensitive and objective: an over-tense attitude to the discussion is inhibiting, but a *laissez faire* attitude can cause unmitigated chaos. At times the teacher needs to be aware that the analysis stage may have to be diverted into another playing stage. Sometimes the argument needs a live illustration of what is being implied. There is little time within a role-play session for the teacher to sit back and relax; the 'role' of teacher is at all times challenging.

Setting up a role-play situation

Role-play can involve pairs, small groups of three to five, or a large group of players working on a particular situation. There may or may not be observers of the action. The analysis stage can involve the whole group, or sections of the main group.

Role-play often helps an inhibited group, as they may work out an open-ended situation and then report back their findings in a group discussion. They do not have to become a character and act. It is best to start off informally. You may be chatting over a topic in which the group are generally interested (a feature from the press, or something relevant to their place of work, say). The group may be so stimulated that they respond with lively, conflicting attitudes. When an appropriate moment of conflict occurs, you may well say, 'Let's put that into action and see how we would react in such a situation.' Working in pairs, A represents one side of the argument and B the other. They play it out two or three times. The second time they reverse the roles, and the third time they can return to their original roles. At this point the teacher might like to ascertain if the argument has been modified in any way. As an example, the topic in hand might concern authority. Some people feel that those in positions of authority should be relaxed and on friendly terms with their colleagues—eating in the same dining areas, for example—while others feel that an air of remoteness will establish a more respected relationship. The As might start off by portraying a friendly boss, and the Bs an average type of employee. You will need to decide together on the reasons for the two meeting and where the encounter takes place. After reversing roles, A represents a remote boss, and B again the same employee. After reversing roles again, the discussion is resumed, and the group examine their attitudes in the light of the role-play experience.

When you are giving the group problems to work on, let them involve decision-making as well as being open-ended. For example,

A is the head girl of a school which has a very active school council. A feels that the school would be a more positive place to work in if some of the petty rules were dropped. B is the new head mistress and A feels that she must convince B. Although B is keen to keep up the standards of work within the school, she would like to be considered a progressive headmistress. This particular problem concerns uniform. Does the encounter occur in the head's study, or the sixth-form common room? What is the outcome?

My favourite method of getting good interaction with an inhibited group is to give separate whispered instructions to the As and to the Bs. The As huddle around you, while the Bs remain seated, and you give them very brief but crucial instructions about their roles and the situation. The As return to their places while the Bs are given their brief. The As and Bs meet to play out an encounter. The outcome is discussed.

I find that if I take a role myself within the story or situation I can often encourage the group to become more involved, as well as being able to direct the action from within the confines of the situation. As potential leaders gain confidence, I am able to take a smaller part and merely plant and probe if the action becomes stale.

Once the group has become more relaxed, suggest that one character may do something unexpected but which would, if challenged, still be plausible within the limits of the role. I sometimes play this character if the group are a little lacking in confidence.

If you are role-playing with a fairly experienced group, let someone new take over a role and see if he can sustain the arguments already established.

It is certainly much easier to let the group work in twos and threes, but as you become more experienced you will want to experiment with situations using larger groups, and perhaps the whole group. When using the whole group, the numbers of players involved can be limitless as long as there is a role for each one. It helps to write brief character notes on cards and then distribute these, so that each person has an initial brief. The room should be set so that the group knows the layout of the place, where they are to meet (e.g. is it at work, at home, or somewhere else?). Try to take situations with which the group are familiar and have experienced in some way. The topics might be concerned with incompatibility between colleagues at work, failure of local government to provide sufficient houses, misunderstanding between a travel agent and his clients, and so on. But have confidence in your group and let them supply you with ideas. It is then up to you to search for a theme, and thus help them to gain more understanding of their own lives. Role-play methods can quite often be scheduled into a programme of work related to a subject (e.g. history, social studies, geography), or within a course on anything from management techniques to personnel work.

Once you have found various structures to use, you will soon find it quite easy to take an idea from a discussion and present it as a problem to be actively explored. Role-play helps people to modify their own attitudes and opinions, so that they are able to assess situations a little more objectively. If we want to create understanding between people, one way to set about it is not by formal explanations, but by letting attitudes arise from the action.

Games

During the last few years there has been much experimentation with children's games, both educationally and in the theatre. They can be a very valuable aid to introducing a group to drama; they should however be used with discretion and selected with discrimination.

If I am going to use a game, I try to sort out the reason for using it—for instance, I might have a problem with a particular group and hope that a certain game will help to overcome the problem. Problems might arise from a very lively group who need to channel energy by doing something fast and exhausting; a group who find concentration difficult; a group who need help in overcoming diffidence, or whose members find it very difficult to integrate and need a common interest.

On the other hand the game might be a useful introduction to the theme the group are going to explore. The game need not always precede the session as a 'warm-up'; it is often worth while using a game or exercise during a session either to help make a particular point or to help change an atmosphere. I have found that sometimes, during a long rehearsal session, some of us may get a bit giggly and find it difficult to concentrate, or we have been working on a very tense situation and need to relax, and that the solution is to use an appropriate game.

There are two excellent reasons for using games with children when you first take them for drama: children enjoy games and therefore initial tension is broken down; nearly every child understands that to gain maximum enjoyment from a game you must adhere to its specific rules and co-operate with the other players. In

this way they gain self-control and thus confidence, and the game
has encouraged group participation.

'Hunt and Hunter' (see description opposite) was my salvation
with one class of very naughty thirteen-year-olds. There were thirty
of them, and they were backward. Each week they announced that
drama was stupid. I had tried most things unsuccessfully and was
reluctant to go ahead with other ideas until there was some degree of
group integration and co-operation. At the end of yet another
unsatisfactory lesson, I suggested that everyone got a chair and
made a circle. I then described the game briefly, and produced two
muslin blindfolds. We played the game the first time with a great
deal of ritual. When all the shuffling and fidgeting had stopped, I
said in a very loud, deep, slow voice, 'The game has started.' Once
the group had begun to enjoy the tensions and formalities of this
game, these words were a magic reminder that shuffling and fidgeting must cease, otherwise the excitement lost its intensity.

It is well worth while being conversant with the rules of a good
selection of games suitable for various occasions. I have collected
most of mine from teachers' courses, books of party games (see book
list, page 136), and from children. I've also found it useful to adapt a
party game to a more relevant setting; for instance, 'The Family
Coach' can become 'The Family Caravan', and a marvellous game
called 'The Dragon and the Princesses', from *Party Games for Children*
(compiled by Mary Vivian), can be turned into an escape game
concerning the Berlin Wall and renamed 'East and West' (described
on pages 57–9).

It is useful to collect your games methodically under various
headings. To give details of the many different games would fill
another book, so I shall list a few under different headings and
suggest that you find out the rules either from your group or from a
book of games. The rules for 'Hunt and Hunter' and 'East and West'
are included below.

To encourage concentration, absorption, control
'Keeper of the Keys', 'Minefields', 'Secret Leader', 'Winking Killer',
'Dead Soldiers'.

For channelling energy
'Touch', 'Rooks and Ravens', 'Simon Says'.

To encourage group co-operation, integration
'The Family Coach', 'Hunt and Hunter' (see below), 'Throwing
Faces' (see page 46).

To encourage speech
'Associations', 'I like . . .', 'You mustn't say "yes", and you mustn't
say "no"'.

To overcome lethargy
'I dare you . . .', 'Grandmother's Footsteps', 'Stick-in-the-Mud'.

'Hunt and Hunter'   Everyone sits on chairs or stools in a large circle. The greater the diameter of the circle, the greater fun the game will be. Warn the players that the success of the game depends on total silence and stillness from the onlookers. They must control all shuffling and whispering, and stifle all giggles.

Two people are selected, one as the Hunter and the other as the Hunted. They are blindfolded by two helpers, who take them to opposite sides of the circle and turn each player round three times. The helpers then return to their places.

The game starts when there is complete quiet, and the teacher says in an 'imposing' voice (to build up the ceremony), 'The game has started.' The two protagonists then start to move. The Hunter should be encouraged to listen for the whereabouts of the Hunted so that he can more easily catch his victim. They must both keep moving while the game is in progress, and it is the duty of the rest of the group to steer the players gently back into the circle if they move towards the edges. The drama can be increased by suggesting that the Hunter utters a huge roar on catching the victim.

As the group becomes proficient, develop the game in various ways. Children enjoy creating their own versions of a well-loved game. I've progressed to suggesting that four people play—two Hunters and two Hunted. The Hunted are allowed to feel each other's faces before the game starts, and the two Hunters are selected from the group when they all have their eyes closed, so that neither of them therefore has any idea who is his ally nor who the victims are. Quite often I abandon the blindfolds as the players enjoy the game sufficiently to want to keep their eyes shut without assistance.

'East and West'—*based on 'The Dragon and the Princesses'*   As this is a game to use with a responsive group, it is worthwhile starting off the session with a discussion. You might begin by mentioning the implications of the Berlin Wall, and find out how much the group knows about it. Perhaps some of them might be able to recall a true escape story connected with the wall.

The group should divide into pairs, A and B. The As move to one half of the room, and the Bs to the other. The As are the Rescuers and the Bs the Relatives behind the wall, with one extra pair acting as Guards. The As build a 'wall' out of chairs, thus dividing the two sections but leaving a gap in the middle of the wall. The Bs are asked to build a set in their space representing the town near the wall.

Relatives imprisoned
behind the Wall (Bs)

Berlin
Wall and
blindfolded
guards

Rescuers (As)

1   *The East and West Game*

They might use a large table to represent a radio station, a high box or cupboard could be the secret code centre, two chairs a bridge over a river. They then select spies to act as look-outs and to see that the Guards do not approach their coding centres. When the whole set has been arranged, the teacher selects the couple who are to be Guards. The Guards are blindfolded and then turned round three times and positioned by the gap in the wall. Then one pair is selected as the first escape team. The Relative, B, is also blindfolded, and the Rescuer, A, has to make his way deftly past the blindfold guards to the other side of the wall, and then bring B back through the gap to safety. The Guards must try to catch the pair. They can only achieve this by luck and by listening to the sound of feet moving. The whole group must be absolutely silent. When a pair is caught that pair becomes Guards. The Guards may only have three chances at catching a fleeing couple.

Extension: Once the group are familiar with the game, they decide who they are, why B wishes to escape, and A devises an elaborate escape route. If the group are very co-operative, organise two couples to escape, and encourage a complicated escape route.

Evaluation

It seems to me vitally important that a group, whether they are young children or adults, should have ample opportunity to evaluate and assess the practical work with which they have been involved. Many people tend to be inhibited and inarticulate because they have not been encouraged to express their views in a positive and perceptive way. This is an area in which a teacher using the drama method can make a valuable contribution. Words and movement are our life-blood, and it is the right of every person to be given the encouragement to master a vocabulary which will enable him to communicate his ideas fluently. There are some people who are never going to be especially proficient at reading or writing, but all of us need to express ourselves through speech; we have to convince others we are worthy of a certain job, prepared to accept responsibility, able to make an adequate spouse, and so on.

If you are working with children or an inarticulate group, you will need to inspire talk not only by talking yourself, thus providing a relevant vocabulary, but also by asking a variety of pertinent questions. If you ask such a group their feelings about a particular piece of work they will respond initially by saying such things as, 'Yes, I liked it', 'Well, you know, it was good, yes, it was good', or 'Oh, it was stupid, boring—that sort of thing is boring.' I quite often try to help an inarticulate group during the first few sessions by giving my own reactions about a piece of work, and my reasons for them, gradually introducing more open-ended questions so that they can agree, disagree or develop my ideas. The following questions, asked at the right moment, are useful for developing critical appreciation:

Did you enjoy watching the scene?

Which parts did you find interesting?

Was your attention held, all or part of the time? Why was or wasn't this so?

Can you give instances of the parts which were enjoyable and those which were not?

Were the words and movements easy to understand? Was the plot and action clear?

Did you believe in the characters? Were they real? In what way?

What was particularly true to life about any particular character (speech, mannerisms, gestures, choice of words, stance)?

Did the characters really listen to each other?

What happens if they all speak at once?

Did the opening work—was interest held at once, and why?

Did the scene build up to a climax? What was the climax?

Was it necessary to have a climax?

Can a scene be interesting if there is no climax?

What type of scene was it (comedy about people or a situation)?

Did we learn something about the way people react?

Was it true to life? Were the incidents well observed?

Did the set help the action? Was it used realistically?

Could we hear what was said?

Was there any masking of important characters when they were speaking or making a significant movement?

Did the players act as a team?

Did they really listen to each other?

Was the mimed action clear? Say when you believed in it.

Always praise and encourage work which shows progress, saying why you feel the work is improving. I find that wholehearted warmth and enthusiasm for work which has taken effort really does pay dividends. If I feel that a person is not doing his best, is not really trying, then I articulate my dissatisfaction formidably. Once he shows signs of involvement, then I am delighted. So many young drama teachers need to learn to be positive in their approach to the work. You must work hard to win sufficient respect from a group to enable you to be friendly, firm, and fair with each person.

3 Material for improvisation

The group exercises and games described in the previous chapter are intended to be used and developed as an introduction to, and useful practice for, work involving imaginative improvisation on any specific topic. Once group members are at ease with one another, as well as able to work individually, you can begin to explore and then experiment with a wide variety of situations and subjects. You will also find that, as the members of the group gain confidence in each other and in you, they will become much more adventurous and will in time be able to improvise the action of anything from vegetable soup to a mountaineering team. Any type of situation is possible with a very aware, imaginative, sensitive group, but you need to realise that the average group will find a certain range of situations and topics more acceptable than others, particularly when these are relevant to their own particular needs. For instance, I have found that some groups work happily with fantasy, whereas others prefer working on a documentary or a miscellany programme of poetry and prose.

Choosing a topic

It is often advisable to start off with a situation which you know many of the group to be familiar with (see pages 83–5). Try to pool suggestions; include both the ones they offer and the ones you are interested in doing. If the group seems particularly keen on any one idea which you may be a little afraid of or dubious about, make an attempt to tackle it. Once a topic has been decided on, I often ask the group a number of questions related to the theme, the situation, the characters, the set, and so on. In this way we all realise that there are more ways than one to explore and present a given situation. Try not to let the discussion get too involved, as this tends to paralyse the action.

When you and your group have made several tentative and then more prolonged explorations into a variety of familiar and known situations, you can try similar experiments with unfamiliar situations and progress to other material such as stories, poems and themes.

For young children, choose subjects which involve plenty of movement, repetition and fantasy. Very simple situations work well—for example, underwater adventures leading to the story of 'The Little Mermaid' by Hans Andersen; a toyshop or toy cupboard coming to life, leading perhaps to the story from the ballet *Coppelia*; nursery rhymes, ballads, and poems such as 'The Pied Piper' and many of A. A. Milne's poems, e.g. 'The King's Breakfast'. Look out for stories with a clear plot, definite characters and plenty of action.

With a more senior group almost any topic or situation is possible, and the method of working on an idea is more important than the choice of idea. Is it to be considered symbolically, realistically or abstractly? Will you work mainly verbally, concentrating on characterisation, or will you choose to work through movement and vocal sound, or will it be a question of marrying the two methods?

I once saw a group of inexperienced adults on a drama course tackle symbolically a well-known English nursery game (Oranges and Lemons). They had only been working together for four days, during which they had been experiencing group games and exercises, but they were able to explore the problem of racial prejudice through the format of the game (one member of the group was a West Indian teacher). They had a day in which to explore the situation. Once the suggestion had been approved by everyone, they worked out the theme through ritual movement, chants and stylised actions. Simple orange and yellow paper masks were made to help identification and to complete the stylised effect. By the end of the afternoon the group were prepared to show their interpretation to the rest of the course.

The initial approach

When preparing work for a particular session, you must again consider the needs of the group, as well as the ideas you are going to explore together. The group may need to work on skills and techniques in order to develop a better vocabulary of expression involving the use of the body, voice and imagination. If they need help in unblocking the imagination, appropriate games or exercises at the start of the session will help them to realise the theme they are preparing. They may need exercises to encourage better group integration, or they may like a lively start to some strong warm-up music or a vigorous game to banish lethargy; conversely, they may enjoy a very concentrated start that helps them to focus their attention on the work.

The exercises described in Chapter 2 can be used to satisfy most of these needs; but as you become more proficient as a teacher, you will be able to adapt and experiment with various versions of the exercises to suit a particular group.

When working with a known and realistic situation, it is worth trying out some of the following approaches:

1 Let the set, characters and action evolve from the start; for instance—'We've decided to turn the room into an airport. Who are you, why are you here, what are you doing, and what section of the airport are you moving through, working in, and so on?' You might play a record to help the group initially. Every so often, stop the action to sort out details of set, characters and action. Finally, from the different happenings, develop together a sequence of actions. There need not necessarily be a grand climax.

2 To start with, work out with the group the details of set and characters. Probe into the characterisation, letting members decide why they are at that particular place at that particular time, their attitude to the place, to other characters and to the things they are involved in doing. Then, when the action starts, everyone has a clear idea of the place and of who he is, why he is there, and what he is doing. The action might start in mime, and you could then stop it to discuss the developments, and add improvised talk. After this, various happenings will begin to occur which can be put into a sequence of action.

3 Similar preparation to 2, but this time start the group off as a still photograph which slowly comes to life. You might then suggest that one section remains active while the rest freeze, followed by general action, followed again by a small section working while the main group are 'frozen' once more. Sometimes it is interesting to choose a photograph or picture postcard and decide on a situation which might lead to the incident or scene depicted, thus concluding the improvisation with the group as a still replica of the picture.

If the situation is based on the unknown or fantastic, it is interesting to let the group work on stylised movement with added vocal sounds (see pages 49–50). The sound and movement patterns which evolve from these exercises can lead to strange and powerful improvisations connected with jungles, underwater, space, the human body, and so on.

Exercises for character exploration (pages 40–51) can often lead to a topic for experiment for once the group have created a set of characters for themselves they are then keen to think of places and situations in which these characters might meet and interact. Take, for instance, five characters in wartime, all in the same service. Where do they meet? How do they establish relationships? What happens? Is the final happening based on an external situation or an internal relationship problem? With the whole group, you could suggest that they are people connected with the same organisation, club, or firm. They might all be cleaners in a large office, members of a football team, bus-drivers and so on—encourage the group to make suggestions. It is helpful if you give an exercise to work on as individuals which encourages the development of the personal details and idiosyncracies of the character. Once the majority of the characters are formed, work out what they are doing, why they are there, how they interact. Among plays which have given me good ideas for characterisation are *Journey's End* by R. C. Sherriff, and *The Changing Room* and *The Contractor* by David Storey.

A teacher can sometimes help a different group to cope with material which initially might seem too demanding, by telling an open-ended story in which members of the group participate as it is told. Each person in the group becomes the main character in the story and moves to the action as it is suggested. The story can start with a known situation and character type, and can include a dream or flashback sequence. Once the group seem absorbed in the action, let the story stop and let them complete it on their own. To start with this can be done as a group exercise, but eventually it can be an exercise worked out by sets of two or three people.

Story-telling

I thoroughly enjoy telling stories but have not always been very lucky with the improvisations arising from the story-telling. Quite often the story is justified as an end in itself, and the group are only interested in hearing yet another tale. Even with encouragement and some pushing, the improvisations resulting from the story have often been lethargic and rather wooden. I have found that the following method helps to combat this reaction and encourages spontaneity and a refreshing re-interpretation of the original story.

Having selected a story, I spend some time considering games or exercises which might be related to some aspect of the plot and theme. We work on these before the story-telling. By doing this, each person in the group is helped to relate imaginatively, personally and physically to the story as it is told, rather than just imaginatively and mentally. At the end of the story-telling everyone

Asking for ideas

is more prepared to translate the narrative into action, and the results are likely to be more lively, spontaneous and vivid.

Try to memorise the basic plot of the story you have chosen and re-tell it in your own words. If you forget part of the original or leave out a character, you will simply have to improvise spontaneously. It is as well to look out for stories that have a strong, clear, simple plot upon which the group may improvise and elaborate, with scope for incidental development of character and action; a variety of characters or objects; and plenty of action which involves the whole group. You can also look out for stories that can be easily divided into sections, or those which would be suitable for work with sets (e.g. a harbour, boats and sailors, the sea, an underwater world).

Here is a step-by-step example of the method described above, used for an improvisation based on the Norwegian folk tale, *Peter, Paul and Espen* (see pages 132–4).

1 Before telling the story, prepare one or two introductory sessions which might include:
  (*a*) a series of journeys (see pages 38–9);
  (*b*) character building—choose some of the stock character types in the story and let everyone experience these types in turn, e.g. a weary old man or woman; a lazy, careless youth; a greedy bully; a bright, enthusiastic youth; a spoilt princess; a dignified leader—see pages 40–4;

2   *A river (group formation using scarves)*

(c) situations for the different characters, such as a mime of get-
    ting up in the morning, a mime showing what he or she enjoys
    doing and does not enjoy doing; a problem for the character to
    solve in mime (e.g. chopping down a tree, preparing supper);
    or situations which bring the characters into contact with one
    another.

2 Work on incidents related to the story.
  Suggest that the whole group improvise the activities of a Norwegian fishing village: it is early summer, the spring snows have
  at last melted, people are preparing for summer.
      Three people prepare for a journey. A is enthusiastic, B is lazy,
  C is bossy. How do the three cope with the journey through a
  great forest, glacier country, a swelling river, over a steep moun-
  tain? How can the forest, the boulders, the river be created by the
  group as a whole? Let small groups be involved in some of the
  suggested ideas.

3   *A tree (formed by three people and a hoop)*

Let small groups work on the idea of a tree which shoots up an extra branch every time it is cut by an axe. Encourage the use of movement and vocal or percussive sound.

3 Narrate the story to the group. Then let the group help you divide it into scenes which can be dramatised. For this particular story I have found the following plan useful:

(a) The village—introductory movement and mime to show different activities, arrival of the herald, reaction of the old man and his sons to the news.

(b) The journey—the forest, rocks and boulders, the river, arrival at the palace.

(c) Outside the place—queue of woodcutters, the royal party, the king's announcement, cutting the tree, punishment of the elder brothers, Espen's good fortune (or was it?).

As a follow-up, it might be worth relating the story's ending (happiness through riches or a beautiful royal wife) to modern incidents such as winning the football pools, or a beauty contest.

Before casting the characters, ask the group for suggestions. If you are working with a small group it may be necessary to give people more than one part.

4 Work through the whole story in mime. Then take each section and work through it with improvised dialogue.

5 Break off frequently, after a sequence of action, and discuss the results: Was the story clear? Were the characters real? Are we beginning to believe in them? What do we wish to convey about the atmosphere of the village?—about the people who live in the village?—about the main characters? How can the action be improved? (Try out one or two suggestions.)
    Did the last suggestion make it better, and why?
6 As the action and characters begin to take shape, suggest that props, hats, scarves and perhaps sound effects are gradually added.
7 Finally, either you can polish and prune ready for a 'showing', or you may feel that the group has gained sufficient satisfaction from a good run-through involving you and each other.

Both with children and with adults, the response to this story has been enthusiastic. The groups have enjoyed the contrast of being objects and set as well as characters. Some groups have worked out exciting movement patterns for the journey, adding their own vocal and percussive sound accompaniment. Groups have ranged from a class of thirty-two children to one of only eight adults. It has been encouraging to see how both children and adults can use their initiative together with imagination to reproduce the story in their own terms.

Group story-telling

This method of story-telling is usually successful when the group is willing to work together as a whole. Stories are made up spontaneously and will vary a lot in both quality and length. The number of people taking part may range from a whole group through sets of four or five down to pairs.

Sequence 1—Stories from a word sequence

The teacher starts off the proceedings, with the group sitting round in a circle. The leader says a word—for example, 'sunset'; the next person goes on, 'Sunset reminds me of . . .' and then adds a word which he associates with sunset; the game continues round the

Loading the ship

circle, each person adding an associated word to the previous one. Try to avoid pauses and repetition, and keep to nouns.

A story can be built from one word; again the teacher starts off with a word, and then each person in turn adds a suitable word so that a simple and logical statement is built up. A group of ten might produce: 'The old man went out into the wintry cold night.' Repeat exercise several times to give everyone confidence in his utterances.

Once sufficient confidence has been instilled, suggest that each person adds a phrase of several words or a sentence to the round. It is at this point that the stories can develop and deepen, although sometimes there is disappointment when a promising section is 'thrown away' by someone who has run out of ideas, has not been concentrating on the previous narrative, or finds the method too difficult.

If a story is created and proves suitable for improvisation, let the whole group or smaller sets experiment with it by using action.

Sequence 2—Stories from simultaneous narration and action

Try having the group sitting in a horseshoe shape. Suggest that some members might like to become characters or objects from the story about to be improvised. If so, these people should move into the space and improvise with mime or movement as the story develops. You may find that the story-tellers often feel more committed to the logical sequence of the plot once actors are involved.

Experiment with the story-tellers providing narration and thus keeping the action moving, and the actors improvising the words of the characters, objects, and so on in the story. The group must work very sensitively and co-operate well at this point. The plot sequence is dependent on both the narrators and the actors helping each other to extend the action logically.

As a variation, divide the group into sets of three to five. Each person in turn provides the narration while the rest act out the story, adding dialogue, sound effects, as seems suitable.

Sequence 3—Three little words

Suggest that each member of the group writes down, on three separate pieces of paper, the names of a character, a place and an object. (Sometimes it is fun to suggest a particular theme or type of story to start with, such as a fairy story, a Western, a tale of gang-sters.) The pieces of paper are then put together in three piles and each pile is well shuffled. Groups of three to five people are formed; one person from each group takes a piece of paper from each pile and the groups then create a story around the character, place and object named on the slips of paper. Encourage the groups to let the story evolve from spontaneous improvisation rather than having too much initial discussion, which can paralyse subsequent action.

Sequence 4—Stories from sounds and music

Sounds Let everyone find a space on his own and sit down. Then explain that a sound will be made by something in the room, and that all must listen to it with eyes shut and imagine what it could represent and, perhaps, how it could be introduced into a sequence of action, like the soundtrack of a film. When all eyes are shut, you make the first sound—something simple, such as a pen knocking against a piece of wood. Repeat the sound several times, allowing time for imagination to work. Then ask everyone to open his eyes, and find out what happened.

Encourage detailed replies and, if a very original idea is suggested, give it plenty of encouragement. Suggest that other people then make a sound in the same way, using a variety of objects.

Divide the group into sets, and let each set invent a sound pattern. This can then be recorded on tape and the speed varied to give a different interpretation. If you wish to experiment with movement, suggest that one set provides the sound and a second group listens to it and then responds to it with movement. If a tape recorder is being used, each set can make up a sequence of movement to its own sound played back to them.

This may be developed by suggesting a theme to the whole group, such as hunger, violence, good and evil. Each small set takes an aspect of the main theme and provided an appropriate sound and movement sequence. These are then welded together to give a group interpretation of the theme.

Sound patterns can also be made from vocal rhythms using a word or words and repeating them in rhythmical form, also adding action to complete the pattern.

A theme or topic is decided upon and each person thinks of a word, sentence, or phrase associated with it. These are then worked into a rhythm—for example, slow/fast/slow or loud/quiet/quiet. The movement interprets the words and the rhythm. The whole group may then be blended together. This can be an interesting way of starting an improvisation, and it can also lead on to sound poems involving action.

Music Play a short but complete piece of music to stimulate a mental image. The group should listen with their eyes shut. Then replay the piece and suggest that each person invents a story which suits the music, and which he will then mime to the music; or that small sets work out a story between them to fit the music.

If you are working with recorded music, it will be useful for students to develop a vocabulary of expression-movement. Encourage this by suggesting that they move in an appropriate manner to each different piece of music you play to them—e.g. very slow and sinuous; light, quick and gay; heavy and ponderous; jerky and staccato; and so on. Even an inexperienced teacher can do this quite easily if he has a natural interest in music and is prepared to listen to a wide variety and build up a collection of tapes and records.

Sequence 5—Stories from objects

Make a collection of various objects, some unusual and some familiar, which can be held in the hand. Have the group sitting in a circle, so that the objects can be passed round. You might like to suggest that all shut their eyes first, and then each member has to guess what object he is holding only by the sense of touch. Each member of the group then invents a story involving the object he is holding. The stories may be told in turn, as people feel inclined to volunteer; or, if the group is diffident, the stories could be written down.

If you have a fluent group, suggest that one person starts a story which involves his object; the next person continues the story, but must include *his* object, and so on. If this is a little too difficult, the objects can all be placed in front of the group and, as the story progresses, a different object must be introduced by each successive story-teller. It is easier if people volunteer a section at random rather than in strict rotation; this encourages a more spontaneous involvement and the end-product is likely to be fresh and vivid.

Small groups may now be formed and each given one or more objects (for instance a suitcase, a mask, a piece of driftwood) which should feature prominently in a scene improvised around them.

Sequence 6—Stories from costumes

(See Chapter 4, pages 91–105, for making improvised sets and costumes.)

Let everyone wear a costume he has made from waste material and begin to move in a manner which suits his costume. Gradually suggest that costume and movement bring to mind a character. Ask people about the characters they are creating, with questions such as: 'How does your character stand still, sit down, move fast, move slowly? Where does your character spend most of the day? How would your character cope with a task he or she does not want to do? Does your character have any secrets?'

Once all seem involved in their newly created characters, suggest that each person goes over to someone whose costume and character might be linked with his own. Encourage the formation of groups of two, three or four and the creation of a story based on the characters in each group. It might again be necessary to pose various rhetorical questions to help them get started, such as: 'Have any of the characters met before? If so, when, where and why?' A scene could then be worked out showing the first meeting or contact between them.

Simple sets could be constructed to give more atmosphere and theatrical content to the improvisation.

Sequence 7—Stories from 'between the lines'

Choose a well-known ballad, fairy story or nursery rhyme; it should have scope for a good many supplementary characters, even though the main protagonists are few. Suggest that the group find out all they can about the life history of the characters, the neighbourhood they lived in, the reaction of their friends and relatives to the main event in the story. Here is an example, using the nursery rhyme, 'Jack and Jill'. Encourage the group to improvise answers to the following questions, and let one question lead to others which the group might ask one another.

Where did Jack/Jill live—and with whom?

What did they like/dislike doing?

When did Jack first meet Jill? How did they get on?

If they lived in a village, what sort of village was it? What did the people there do for a living?

Was there another source of water for the village?

How did the old people manage to get water from the hill, if this was the only source?

Were there other people using the well when Jack and Jill arrived?

Why did they go together to the well? Was it planned?

Did anyone see Jack fall? What caused him to fall, and how did he fall?

Were there many other, similar accidents on the hill?

What happened after Jack's accident? How did the village react?

Was anyone sued after the accident? Did the well and the hill belong to an individual or to an official body?

What happens if you are knocked over in the street, either in the roadway or on the pavement or sidewalk? Who is responsible? What happens about accidents at work?

This rhyme might very well provide an introduction or link item in an improvised documentary on accident prevention. The topic can cover a wide range of material, particularly if you and your group take cuttings from newspapers, find out about insurance policies, or do some local research into accidents in your area.

Story-telling material

The following list of stories provides a small selection of suggested material for improvisation, at least some of which should be easily available to most readers. A vast range of stories for drama can be found in legends, myths, folk tales, fables, the fairy tales of other countries, historical stories, Bible stories, as well as in newly published short stories for adults and in some excellent children's fiction, and you will be able to add to this list with ideas and discoveries of your own. The first twelve stories below are suitable for young children. For infants I would suggest nursery rhymes and simple fairy tales like *Red Riding Hood*, *Goldilocks* or *Hansel and Gretel*. Children, particularly the under-eights and those who are less able, need to know the story very thoroughly. Adults can often make a beautiful interpretation of a very simple children's story.

(Publishers' names have not been supplied where a story exists in many different editions. Bibliographies from the National Book League, 7 Albemarle Street, London, W1X 4BB, can help in the finding of suitable material.)

The Little Mermaid by Hans Christian Andersen—mimed movement of the sea, fishes, underwater plants, spells, strange sounds and noises, walking on different surfaces.

Snow White and the Seven Dwarfs—stock characterisation, mirror movement, spells, group movement as a forest, chorus effects.

Gulliver's Travels by Jonathan Swift—seeing the world from the point of view of a very small person, then of a giant; mimed movements of a very small and a very large person.

Alice in Wonderland by Lewis Carroll—floating dream movement, changing from big to small, animal movements, scene in court.

Coppelia—puppet movement, stock characterisation, group dancing (especially based on traditional or country dances), searching for a lost object.

Chanticleer and the Fox (*The Nun's Priest's Tale*) by Geoffrey Chaucer and *Uncle Remus* by Joel Chandler Harris—animal characterisation and movement, lively dialogue for improvisation.

The Iron Man by Ted Hughes (Faber)—mechanical movement.

Pandora's Box (Greek legend)—flexible for adaptation; writhing movement sequences, vocal sound effects.

The Remarkable Rocket by Oscar Wilde (in *Fairy Tales* by Oscar Wilde, published by the Bodley Head)—link with a firework celebration.

Borrobil by William Croft Dickinson (Penguin Books: Puffin)—good group movement; personification of winter and spring and the subsequent battle between them; imaginative description of St George and the dragon.

The Goblin Spider by Philip Payne (in *Legend and Drama*, Book 2, published by Ginn)—warriors, spells, mimed movement to portray stickiness, a strange journey, fight with a monster spider.

Legends: *King Midas*, *Medusa*, *The Sleeping Beauty*, stories of Norwegian Trolls—excellent for control: characters are turned to stone or metal, or are put to sleep.

The Story of the Prodigal Son, from the Bible—well worth modernising (could also be a prodigal daughter); verbal improvisation as well as movement sequences.

I am David by Anne Holm (Methuen, and Penguin Books: Puffin) —excellent escape sequences.

The House of the Nightmare and Other Eerie Tales edited by Kathleen Lines (Heinemann Educational, and Penguin Books: Puffin) these stories should be retold in your own words; the volume includes 'The Monkey's Paw'.

The Soldier and Death by Arthur Ransome—good for a large group production; includes a journey, crowd scenes, court scenes, devils.

The Pardoner's Tale by Geoffrey Chaucer—clear-cut character work, provokes lively dialogue and improvisation, crowd scenes.

Mak the Shepherd from the Wakefield Cycle of Mystery Plays—good for Christmas; encourages good characterisation, lively dialogue and improvisation, has an excellent chase sequence.

The Pilgrim's Progress by John Bunyan—a stimulating project for modernisation; good for characterisation, clear cut argument.

The Metamorphosis by Franz Kafka (Penguin Books)—difficult, but worth attempting with a serious, involved group.

Shakespeare's plays—re-tell them as simply as possible; improvisation can either be in period or modernised.

Nineteenth-century melodramas, *Maria Marten* and *Sweeny Todd, the Demon Barber of Fleet Street*—fun to refer to for ideas if you are going to improvise a melodrama.

For eerie or surrealistic stories, look also at the work of Edgar Allen Poe and Roald Dahl (particularly *Kiss, Kiss*, published by Penguin Books).

Poems

Look out for poems of the following kinds: narrative poems in the
third person (on the whole, poems in the first person do not work
well); descriptive poems (narrative or lyrical) which lead to movement patterns arising from the flow of words; and poems which give
scope for improvisation. Do not neglect the old favourites such as
'The Pied Piper', 'The Ancient Mariner', 'The Hunting of the Snark',
'Tarantella', just because they *are* old favourites.

Try to use a poem differently with each new group; you might aim
to obtain a slightly different visual or vocal emphasis each time.
Again, encourage the group to make suggestions as to how the
poem might be explored, and work from their ideas.

Here is a suggested plan for working with a poem which is to be
spoken and moved to simultaneously:

1 It sometimes helps to divide your group into three sections—Section A, the light voices; Section B, the medium voices; and Section
   C, those with dark, deep voices (usually men). The group will
   enjoy helping to decide whose voice belongs in which category. It
   is advisable to let each person read a couple of lines before the
   decision is made. The group can now work as a choir, experimenting with the different-toned sections to provide interesting har-
   mony patterns. (This can take time!)

2 Before reading the poems to the group, try working with some of
   the ideas you have abstracted from it; for instance, for T. S. Eliot's
   poem 'Skimbleshanks' you might start off with an improvisation
   based on the activities in a railway station, and another session
   might be concerned with the movement and different per-
   sonalities of cats. The group can often provide plenty of factual
   material.

3 Read the poems to the group and then find out if they would like
   to explore it a little more. If they are not happy with it, find out
   why. Be prepared to forgo using it. (If you have a critical group, I
   suggest you go prepared with several contrasting poems.)

4 Distribute a stencilled copy of the poem to each person. (This
   could be done before reading it out, but find out which method
   you prefer.)

5 Now encourage the group to speak the poem together, so that
   everyone gets a 'feel' for the words. You might like to have them
   all moving around as they work through this stage, in which case
   suggest a speed and manner of movement. The faster they move
   and the more complicated the movement, the freer the voices, but
   this only applies to an able group.

6 Thus, from a very basic start, you can ask for suggestions as to how the poem should be spoken—in sections, individual lines, single words.

7 Experiment with different vocal effects—some parts spoken slowly, whispered, echoed, some parts intoned. Work on pauses, play around with individual words which need emphasis, or lines which are significant.

8 If the group becomes involved in these experiments, try working on the poem in movement, and then in movement and speech together—perhaps adding some percussion. Translate the words and rhythms into a sound pattern which shadows the original.

9 Gradually begin to cast the poem to individuals and to small sets within the group—a word, a line, a section. Remember your three-tone choir which you selected earlier.

10 At this stage you may find it necessary to dig around for more ideas to help the interpretation. If so, divide the group up to work on different aspects of the poem.

11 You will know when the right moment has come to shape the work. Again experiment, knowing that you are all free to discard an idea at any time if it seems to jar with the general shape. Sometimes a marvellous idea which evolved from an improvisation session fails to ignite during the polishing stage; if this happens, get rid of it. This is the time to be objective and encourage others in the group to be likewise. I have often been reluctant to throw out a good idea, but have been persuaded to do so by the reasoning of the group.

12 Always finish a session with criticism. Encourage the group members to say what they thought was good about the work and why, and let them think out any improvements with which they are prepared to experiment. By encouraging positive criticism you are helping the group to look at their work more objectively and to be more perceptive, imaginative and sensitive.

Improvising round a poem

The following poem, and the description of a session based upon it, would be suitable for children aged nine and over.

THE CHANT OF THE AWAKENING BULLDOZERS
We are the bulldozers, bulldozers, bulldozers,
We carve out airports and harbours and tunnels.
We are the builders, creators, destroyers,
We are the bulldozers, LET US BE FREE!
Puny men ride on us, think that they guide us,
But WE are the strength, not they, not they.
Our blades tear MOUNTAINS down,
Our blades tear CITIES down,
We are the bulldozers,
NOW SET US FREE!
Giant ones, giant ones! Swiftly awaken!
There is power in our treads and strength in our blades!

We are the bulldozers,
Slowly evolving,
Men think they own us
BUT THAT CANNOT BE!

Patricia Hubbell

First, ask how many of the children have looked at a building site or even, perhaps, been on one. Find out where, what was going on, what tools were used.

Suggest that everyone finds a place in the room on his own, and that he then puts into action one of the activities he saw on the building site. When the activities have been worked out, ask for explanations of a few of them. Everyone should then become an object on the site and freeze into shape. Let the children relax, and ask what they were representing.

Next, get them to work in pairs, with A as the worker and B as a tool or piece of equipment which can be operated by one man. They must be well spaced out round the room. Each pair should work as a partnership and should change roles when directed by the teacher. Encourage appropriate sounds to accompany the actions.

Read the poem to the group and ask them for their opinions about it, what it conveyed to them, and so on. Then suggest that they form sets of four and turn themselves into bulldozers. Aim for simulation of the action and movement of the machines. Move round and give encouragement, perhaps asking questions which will help to solve a particular problem. (It is helpful to carry a drum or cymbals in case you wish to capture everyone's attention and make a general comment, or one that is applicable to several different sets.) If any of the sets would like to, let them demonstrate their 'bulldozers' to the rest, and encourage positive criticism. Still in fours, they can then prepare and simulate a crane, or any other large piece of equipment on the building site.

You can now co-ordinate the site. Select one set of four as a bulldozer, another as a crane, and appoint two men to be in charge of these. The rest resume their man-and-tool work in pairs as at the start of the session. You now have workers and equipment.

The equipment remains on the site, quite still, ready to be used by the workmen. The workmen go off to a corner of the room and prepare for coming to work in the morning. Question the group on the way people arrive at work, their different attitudes to work, their work-mates and their equipment.

Let the children in pairs take opposite parts. Encourage them to build up extensions to the action which might involve the whole site or part of the site. Gradually build and deepen the action. Decide on the theme as well as the story from the ideas they produce.

Probe, to find out what is happening. Do not be content with one-word answers. If an accident occurs, find out what type of accident it was, who was responsible, why it happened. How do the workmen get on with the foreman? Is the building firm interested in a good standard of work from its employees? Probe even further for a more fantastic happening—for instance, the machines take over from the men and then decide to go on strike, but the men do not want to strike.

It is particularly important not to supply the development of the action yourself. Children will participate and create much more freely when they see that you are using their ideas. Always try to ask *them* to solve a particular problem, rather than resorting to your own experience and imagination. You will already have enough of a problem in co-ordinating the theme and plot.

Poems to use for improvisation

As with stories listed earlier in this chapter, this is only a small selection of ideas, and you will be able to choose many others to suit your particular group or the kind of work you want to do. The earlier ones in the list are suitable for children; for the very young use nursery rhymes.

'Sir Brian Botany' by A. A. Milne (*When We Were Very Young*: Methuen)—lively, good for stock characterisation, clear story line.

'Sink Song' by J. A. Lindon (*Bedtime Rhymes*: Ladybird)—useful for voice and movement; lively group work can result.

'The Owl and the Pussycat' by Edward Lear (*The Penguin Book of Comic and Curious Verse*)—excellent for movement, animal characterisation; small groups can work on different interpretations.

'Skimbleshanks: the Railway Cat' by T. S. Eliot (*Old Possum's Book of Practical Cats*: Faber & Faber)—link-up with the improvisations on a railway station; cat movement; encourages expressive voice work.

'The Ballad of Semmerwater' by Sir William Watson (*Solo and Chorus*: Macmillan)—improvisation on the turmoil of a flooded city; this poem can work well as a mime or a dance drama.

'Out of School' by Hal Summers (*Dawn & Dusk*: Charles Causley, published Hodder and Stoughton)—scope for improvisation; a strong lively poem particularly helpful for children with reading problems.

'Daniel Jazz' by Vachell Lindsay (*Voices—The First Book*: G. Summerfield, published Penguin)—needs plenty of energy both from the students as well as from the teacher; a strong rhythm, lively voice and body work; try out some percussion as an accompaniment.

'Tarantella' by Hilaire Belloc (*Collected Verse of H. Belloc*: Everyman's Library, Dent)—a poem overused in the fifties and now not used enough; makes an interesting group production if tackled with imagination; work on vocal sound effects with the words; experiment with whispers, echoes and incantations.

'Children's Crusade 1939' by Bertolt Brecht (*Selected Poems of Bertolt Brecht*: Grove Press Inc., New York)—lots of scope for in depth improvisation; useful for group productions.

'I am not yet born' by Louis Macniece (*Penguin Book of Contemporary Verse*: ed. K. Allott)—encourages imaginative movement; needs a sensitive group and care in the interpretation and speaking.

'Timothy Winters' by Charles Causley (*Voices—The Second Book*:

Penguin)—good for voice work, and an excellent base for improvisation.

'Welsh Incident' by Robert Graves (*Penguin Book of Contemporary Verse*: ed. K. Allott)—encourages detailed characterisation; worth attempting the Welsh accent with a talented group; the open-ended situation can be developed.

'The Schoolmaster' by Yevgeny Yevtushenko (*Selected Poems*: Penguin)—a strong change of atmosphere; variety of voice work needed.

'The Ballad of Molly Magee' by W. B. Yeats (*Collected Poems*: Macmillan)—not too demanding vocally, and good for improvisation.

'Mushrooms' by Sylvia Plath (*Voices—The Second Book*: Penguin)—limited movement but very demanding vocally.

Theme Work

This involves work related to a specific issue or subject, which might be topical or connected with the interests of the group. It is more satisfactory when used for an older group of students who have the ability and insight to explore an idea from a variety of angles and may like to contribute material based on their own experience. Suggestions for preparing a production based on a theme are discussed more fully in Chapter 5.

Having chosen a theme, members of the group with different skills can explore it through improvisation, movement and mime, research in libraries and elsewhere, poetry speaking and writing, song and ballad writing, painting, tape recording, filming and, if the work leads to a production, the organisation of stage management. The group may work as a whole on a movement project, a song-making session, or the like, or in sets for research, filming and recording, improvisation, or in pairs for work on props, costumes, or (again) improvisation.

Useful material for exploring the theme might be found in newspapers, magazines, poems, ballads, folk songs both traditional and modern (some of the lyrics from progressive pop music can be appropriate), recorded conversations with relevant people, novels and plays, paintings and photographs. Encourage everyone to contribute to the collection of ideas.

Try to include as much variety as possible in the treatment of a theme. An endless list of topics could be made, but here are a few suggestions to start you off.

The environment—new buildings and their problems; the difference between life on a new housing estate and in an old town; new highways and the demolition that makes way for them; pollution.

Misfits—outcasts from society through the ages to the present day, people who have been or seem to be ahead of their time. Use poems such as 'Refugee Blues' by W. H. Auden, 'The Telephone Conversation' by Wole Soyinka, and those listed in the previous section by Yevtushenko, Yevgeny and Charles Causley. You might also find useful passages from plays such as *A Night Out* by Harold Pinter, *Antigone* by Jean Anouilh, *Heads* by Howard Brenton.

Relationships—between parents and children at different stages in their lives; between man and woman, man and man, man and animals, people of the same age group, people of different ages; between employer and employees at different periods of history, people from different countries and social groups.

Universal topics—a miscellany of writing (passages of poetry, prose, drama), based on the group's ideas and improvisations about such topics as the sun, war, love, death, growth, advertising, employment, childhood, science fiction, and so on.

A ballad—such as 'Victor' by W. H. Auden, or 'The Ballad of Molly Magee' by Yeats, intercut with improvised conversations from characters mentioned in the poem.

An examination of the life and attitudes of a well-known local character from the past—here first stimulate interest by encouraging research into the background of the character, obtaining photographs and documents, if possible conducting taped interviews with local people, collecting conflicting reports and opinions (the local library may be a useful source of material). If a production evolves from the work, suggest that the cast wear a basic costume and add accessories to indicate the period (see pages 93, 105); members of the group might become involved in making authentic reproductions of these.

I had one lively class of fourteen-year-olds who worked on a rather improbable situation set in a group of municipal allotment gardens. There were sixteen students and each adopted his own very strong and individual character. One was trying to dig down to Australia to visit his relatives; another was trying to grow the smallest vegetable marrow in the world; a third grew only plastic vegetables and flowers; a fourth came each day to measure his beans meticulously; a fifth watched the 'wild life' on his patch through a magnifying glass; and so on. One of them, however, was determined to grow the biggest weed in the world. The other gardeners were furious, as the weed seeded itself regularly each night and its roots were beginning to invade the neighbouring plots, so they decided to take a petition to the Town Hall. Nobody there seemed able to help them, but a journalist became interested, interviewed them, and suggested that they went to see their Member of Parliament at the House of Commons. This visit also proved fruitless; the M.P. was not there. They returned to their gardens to find that the Queen (a symbolic figure represented by an enormous mask on a pole) was visiting the owner of the biggest weed in her kingdom. The gardeners met the Queen, and learned to live with the giant weed and its owner. The group worked on this idea for about six weeks and finally decided to turn it into a lunch-hour production before a small audience.

On another occasion the same students examined the reaction of a group of housewives in a block of flats whose lavatories did not flush properly. Again, each student found a very positive character to work with and identified this character with a name used for a lavatory (the throne, the bog, the powder room, the bathroom, for instance). The theme developed until eventually, after the press had been alerted, the army arrived just as flushing got completely out of hand.

Another fourteen-year-old group were fascinated by the subject of red tape, or apparently meaningless official procedure. They collected all sorts of information from newspapers, relatives, friends, about the problems people face when negotiating with a large organisation. Three girls developed their improvisation into a scripted play (*The Butterdish*) which lasted for about fifteen minutes. An extract from it will be found on page 135.

Situations

It is much more satisfactory, with a new group, to begin by working on known or familiar situations. Students will find it easier to participate with a certain amount of real understanding. Work based on a familiar situation is particularly useful for encouraging occupational mime, day-to-day observation of people and their predicaments, and the assimilation and resolving of personal experience.

Work within a basic structure—it may be modified when necessary, but on the whole it is better to keep to the pattern. This allows for experiment, as time can be apportioned to the sections you want to explore. I would suggest the following structure:

Limber or warm-up—this can include movement starters (see Chapter 2), exercises and games. This initial period of a session helps to encourage group integration and general concentration, as well as helping individuals to relate to the theme and to the aim of the session. You might try some occupational mime or perhaps some animal movement, depending on the situation you are using.

Working out the situation—this can be done with the class as a whole, in pairs, with a variety of partners, or in small groups of, say, three or four. During this period you will probably want to develop the situation so that there is deeper involvement by the group, so introduce an 'extension'. You may be able to develop an idea suggested by a member of the group during the action or in subsequent discussion. For instance, if you are working on the idea of a street-market, one of the group might work as a pick-pocket; someone notices him, and what happens? This is a simple example of an open-ended situation which is explored during the action.

Knitting the situation together—now let the group explore the situation without stopping for discussion. They should work as individual characters in an open-ended situation; at this point the leader can sometimes involve himself in the action as a character and gently provoke the development of a plausible happening.

Come and buy

The picnic

Examples of known situations

Day-to-day occurrences: in local high street, railway station, supermarket, street-market, large store, building site. *Extensions*:
escaped animal, coach party, bomb warning, Customs control,
TV camera team, a storm.

Travel: railway or bus journey, jumbo jet, cross-channel boat, car
journey, hot air balloon, magic carpet, rocket, submarine. *Extensions*: breakdown, hijack, stowaway, highwayman, smugglers,
spies, a chase; personification of vehicles.

Particular places: dentist's/doctor's/vet's waiting room, library, car
park, graveyard. *Extensions*: strange noise, burglars, stock characterisation.

Topical events: floods, fire, pithead disaster, shipwreck, hurricane,
war. Refer to current events which can be explored with the added
stimulus of the group having seen pictures on television news-
reels or read about the incidents in the newspapers. (Sometimes
topical events may be too much concerned with the unknown,
particularly for younger age groups.)

Grand events: processions, marches, ceremonies, investitures, traditional pageantry. Use music, commentaries, masks, effigies on
sticks. (This section should also be used with discretion as for
some people such events are part of the unknown.)

Unknown situations

Experiencing the unknown demands much from the imagination. It is important that the group works sensitively together. Do not be afraid of introducing some of the following topics to young children; they are capable of deep imaginative insight. They are happy to explore fantasy situations, and given encouragement to do so and being stretched in this way, they will be less 'blocked' imaginatively when they get older.

Methods for exploring unfamiliar situations could include movement and mime, slow and quick movement, vocal sounds, percussion and records, dream and nightmare sequences, flashbacks. Try some of the following:

Jungle exploration: animal/insect movements, vocal sounds to suit an animal or an atmosphere; occupational mime—cutting down trees, gathering food, spearing fish. *Extensions*: man-eating plants, a tribe of monkeys, explorers, a hermit (perhaps a war refugee), the 'Mowgli' stories.

Desert exploration: mimed movement on different surfaces, in different temperatures; attempting to reach someone or something which keeps moving away (e.g. a shadow). *Extension*: an oasis, prospecting for oil, a mirage, raid on a caravan.

Fire: sounds of fire, mimed movement of a fire from the moment a spark is dropped on dry material, various ways of making fire, beating out a forest fire, moving as an object which is slowly being burnt. *Extensions*: fire in a house, arrival of fire brigade, fire in a hospital or old people's home. Refer to poems, 'Harriet' from *Struwwelpeter*, 'Matilda' from Hilaire Belloc's *Cautionary Tales*.

Space: slow motion movement, dressing in space suits, moving as strange creatures and plants, inventing a planet language. *Extensions*: landing on distant planet, meeting between inhabitants and explorers; a mysterious discovery.

The body: listening to a heart beating, moving to the rhythm of the heartbeat; mimed movement on different surfaces; small groups becoming different parts of the body, such as the inner ear, the stomach digesting food, the brain functioning like a computer. *Extensions*: travellers inside a giant's body; medicine travelling through different areas of the body and soothing the upset part.

Other topics could include magic islands, chaos and creation, underwater cities, machines. With an open-minded approach, and lively imaginations, there is almost no limit to the possibilities.

4 Space and equipment

A room of your own

In order to achieve meaningful work in drama, your main requirement is an empty space in which you and your group can be as noisy or as quiet as the work demands. The size of the space is very much determined by the size and the needs of the group. For a difficult and uncontrolled group, a large space is not advisable, unless you are an experienced teacher. When I first started to teach I was given a hall to work in; but it had classrooms leading off it, and usually the doors of these rooms were flanked by noisy offenders no longer tolerated by teachers inside; it was also a passageway, with a staircase running up either side of it, and every morning the school dinners were brought through our drama area from the kitchen next door. Eventually, after much perseverance, I managed to get cleared a small classroom right at the top of the building. It was to be kept only for drama. There was a lock-up cupboard, space to pin up posters, notices, pictures on the walls, but only fifteen people could manage to do movement at one time, with the rest sitting and watching. This was rather inhibiting, although after the uproar in the hall it seemed like heaven.

The next school I taught in, at Peckham in London, provided an empty classroom with a lock-up stockroom. The room was excellent, at least to start with, as it was fairly isolated, close to the art department, well lit and well ventilated. This school was, however, raising money to build its own drama workshop—an enormous undertaking, but it was an exciting experience to be part of such an industrious team of staff, parents and children. The workshop, when built, was ideal. The main working space was just the right size for classes of thirty, as well as being suitable for small productions. An audience of over one hundred could be happily seated. The small lighting board (initially a Junior 8, though later on we hoped to have an electronic unit) was placed on a raised platform in one corner of the main space; it was handy to control when taking a class, as there was no difficulty in reaching it to alter the lights or to give advice to the student in charge. We had twenty-four power sockets covering the whole workshop area. The lights could be attached to metal beams placed at six-foot intervals across the width

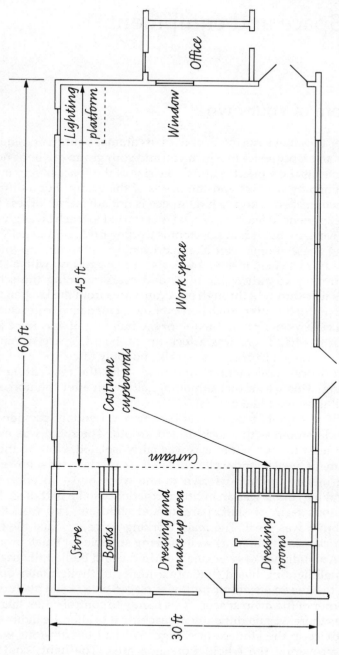

4   *Peckham Drama Workshop*

of the ceiling. These beams also doubled as supports for hanging improvised scenery.

I found that, particularly for older children, the semi-theatrical workshop environment provided an added stimulus for drama work. With younger children I prefer to work in daylight. Down one side of the workshop we had windows which latched open easily, and a double door so that sometimes a class or group could go outside to work. At the far end of the workshop we had storage space consisting of two small dressing rooms, a space for costumes and books, and a store-room with shelves for all the equipment which we quickly accumulated. There was also roof space for large pieces of wood, screens, and so on. In the recessed area at one end we hung a large mirror for make-up, movement and mask work. At the other end of the building was a small office-cum-control room with a window on to the workshop, where we could sit unobserved and watch the students at work. In the building next to the workshop there were washbasins and lavatories, convenient for cleaning faces and hands, and paintbrushes, and for fetching water for such necessities as cups of tea.

I experienced many happy hours working in this 'space'. Since then I have had to use many spaces which, by comparison, have been far from ideal, but for satisfactory work I would stipulate at least that the space is clear of all unnecessary furniture (especially if movement or improvisation is involved in the work); self-contained, fairly isolated and free from distracting noise or other activity; well ventilated, because a drama room can soon smell like a monkey house unless there is a through breeze; and provided with normal acoustics – often a gymnasium is spoilt by echoing acoustics which, combined with ropes to tempt younger groups to emulate Tarzan, make an otherwise good space intolerable. It should also be provided with adequate electric points for record player and tape recorder, and have a reasonable store-room or adequate cupboards for the necessary accumulation of bits and pieces which are collected in the course of drama lessons.

Although lights, rostra blocks, mirrors and other items are well worth having, they are not going to make a mediocre piece of work any better, nor is an excellent piece of work going to be marred without sophisticated apparatus. Admittedly lights can make work visually more attractive, just as electronic equipment can add dimension to sound, but these are superficial niceties which I am delighted to use but am prepared to do without. My aim is to see a group deeply absorbed in a piece of work which is meaningful to them. If this piece of work is later to be used as theatre, we will have then to make the content and characterisation strong enough to hold an audience without the conventional props of the modern stage.

Equipment

The following equipment can be considered when setting up a drama workshop space:

1 Record player and tape recorder; and, if the budget allows, a portable tape recorder as well.

2 Rostra blocks in different shapes and sizes, used to create a set and sometimes to provide a raked area for the audience to sit on.

3 Lighting. This depends a great deal on the space, and whether lights can be slung from batons beneath the ceiling. If not, you may have to use stands, which in my opinion are far too dangerous; I would always prefer to have lights attached to the walls or to a bar secured with a safety chain. Consult a lighting expert as to the number and type of lights you will need. To start with, you will probably manage with about half a dozen fresnel spotlights and a small electronic dimmer board.

4 An overhead projector, excellent for projecting hand-drawn scenery, or other scenic effects, on to a large screen or backcloth (or you can use the larger rostra blocks painted white).

5 An automatic slide projector for photoplays, slides.

6 A manual slide projector if you want to experiment with making 'moving slides. For these you need two squares of lighting gel, cut to fit the slide holder in the projector and glued together on three sides to form a pocket. Put this into the projector with the opening at the top and, using a paint brush, slide into it a little cooking oil, some ready-mixed powder paint and a pinch of baking soda. When the projector is switched on, the heat will activate the mixture so that a swirling coloured image is thrown on to a plain light-coloured wall or even on to plain costumes.

7 A camera, cine-camera and projector.

8 A step ladder for use when fixing lights, hanging scenery, etc.

9 A large mirror fixed to the wall, and also a portable dressmaker's mirror.

10 Display board for notices, pictures, posters, etc.

11 Storage boxes or hampers for props, masks, materials, make-up.

12 Adequate shelf space for books and rails for clothes (hang long clothes on high rail and use the space beneath for storage boxes; get students to collect plenty of wire coat hangers).

13 Stools and chairs (stools are more adaptable). A couple of simple, lightweight tables are useful for painting on, using as a props table, or even as part of the set.
14 Percussion instruments; the minimum would be a tambourine and cymbals.
15 A filing cabinet for all your own reference material.
16 Floor mop, bucket, dustpan and brush.
17 Some people like to have an old carpet which the group can use when they need to come together for discussion. You could of course make one out of clean sacks with the edges bound. I have seen a round mat used most successfully.
18 A typewriter, telephone and electric kettle are always useful.

Materials

The following can be acquired at little or no cost:
Scrap or waste material of all kinds
Newspaper
Cardboard boxes, all sizes (the large ones in which goods such as cookers are packed are ideal for sets)
Cardboard rolls—from stores selling rolls of fabric or lino
Paper bags, all sizes; garbage bags, both paper and plastic
Old sheets, for back projection and costumes
Disused material from window displays in local stores
Unused hoarding advertisements, leftover paper from printers, odd pieces of wallpaper
Packaging of all kinds, including chunks of polystyrene
Off-cuts of fabric from a local factory (if possible)
Lengths of wooden planking or timber offcuts; old ladders, hat racks, laundry hampers, pieces of chicken wire, old wooden hoops, rubber tyres, etc.
Hats, and other accessories such as walking sticks, handbags, spectacles, from jumble (rummage) sales

As make-up is very expensive, try to accumulate a collection of disused lipsticks, eye make-up, foundation, etc.

Materials which need to be budgeted for:

Paintbrushes (assorted sizes)
Paint—start with primary colours
String, rope and wire
Pins and thumb tacks
A good glue (e.g. PVA adhesive)
Scissors—cheap and not too sharp
Adhesive tape

Sugar paper, tissue paper, hard card, shiny gummed coloured paper

Butter muslin in large quantities for sets and costumes

Cane—generally referred to as split cane

A stapler

Chicken wire

Calico, hessian, canvas and plastic sheeting

Coloured gel for lights

Fibre pens

Stage make-up

5 (a)   *Basic costume (loose trousers and tee shirt)*
(b)   *Basic long tunic*
(c)   *Slip-on shawl over basic long tunic*
(d)   *Simple shawl made from a square of material*
(e)   *Short tunic with looped side fastening*

(Split cane can be ordered from a handicraft supplier in different thicknesses in lengths of about 3 metres—10–12 feet—and is flexible enough to form a variety of shapes; see Figure 9.)

For day-to-day improvising, invest in a variety of fabric lengths which do not fray and which can be draped and hung on people. Look out for bright colours which can be machine-washed. Young children love dressing up in old clothes, but as they get older they find cast-off garments less appealing. We had a small dressing room filled with old costumes, dresses, and other garments, but the older students nicknamed it 'the itch room' and eventually we threw everything out.

You will also need an enormous supply of safety pins, elastic bands, clips, needles and thread, and labels (useful for name tags to attach to coat-hangers when the groups are involved in a production).

Costume

Assuming that you are working on a limited budget, and that the production is based on experimenting with ideas worked on in improvisation, there are two types of costume you can consider—conventional (but not formal), or abstract made mainly from scrap or waste materials.

The conventional costume should be designed in a neutral, basic shape which can be used on different occasions with alternative accessories. With older groups I began by dressing the cast in dark trousers, skirts and shirts; and with children I used tights as the basis for costume. I have since found that dark clothes are not very compatible with an inventive lighting plot, and tights are expensive and, if insisted upon, can cause self-consciousness unless the group is very movement-orientated. I now try to work out a costume which is fairly up-to-date, but adaptable. For one production we dressed the entire cast in light grey, loose trousers with elastic waistbands, very easy to make, and we dyed white tee-shirts to match. This basic attire was flexible, virtually unisex, and was approved of by those with bulky proportions as well as by the bird-like figures. On various later occasions we added to it loose, straight or flared tabards, made out of brightly-coloured lining fabric; tie-dyed tee-shirts; and shawls made from squares of lining fabric. The advantage of grey material is the way in which it reflects and absorbs the light.

Another useful acquisition for the costume cupboard is long circular skirts made from heavy material—curtain fabric is effective. If the skirts are left open down one side with strips of upholstery fasteners stitched from waist to hem they can then double as cloaks and can be draped and fastened in a variety of ways. I've found that a costume store full of basic trousers, skirts, tops, scarves and hats is much more useful and usable than the formal, traditional style of costume associated with a scripted three-act play. A simple garment is so much more stimulating to the imagination of both actor and audience.

Abstract costumes tend on the whole to be disposable, as they are often made from waste materials which have little durability. You might devote a drama session to improvising costumes from scrap materials, including some of the following: wooden gym hoops, mesh vegetable bags, newspaper, lengths of plain fabric draped and pinned, silver foil (perhaps secured over a petticoat hoop made from wire coathangers), cane and muslin; boxes—attached to arms, worn on the head or body; cardboard shapes cut to suit different characters and attached to the body front and back, large paper bags appropriately painted; wood shavings glued to muslin or cardboard (excellent for a wig or a rather sculptured beard).

For ways of working with and exploring the potential of these costumes, see 'Stories from costumes', pages 72–3.

Masks

Some of the most interesting mask sessions I have been involved in have occurred when we have made and worked with the masks during the same session. The length of the session is important; you will need at least an hour if you are using masks made from newspaper or paper bags. Here are some suggestions for making masks:

Paperbags   Suggest that each member of the group finds a brown paper bag, preferably free of print, which fits comfortably over the head and can be easily removed. Then provide felt pens (perhaps limiting the colour to black) and let everyone draw on his bag a nose, or a mouth, accenting only one feature. Two tiny eye-holes must also be made to enable the wearer to see out. If the session is short, people could decorate their bags before they come to it, but again you should tell them the particular way you want this done (e.g. with added paper hair, or with features made from shiny coloured paper, etc.).

6   Costume created from newspaper
7   Paper sack costume (may be painted)

8 (a)   Carrot bag costume
  (b)   Patchwork tunic

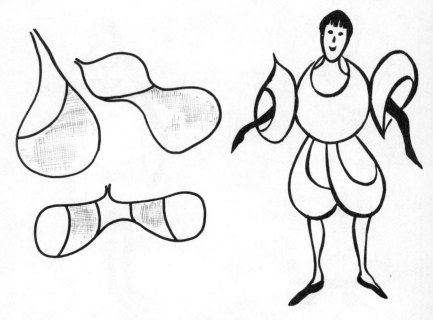

9 (a)   *Stretched muslin over cane shapes*
   (b)   *Cane and muslin costume*

10   *Simple masks*
   (a)   *Box mask*   (b)   *Stick mask*
(c)   *Mask made from packaging from a tennis racquet*
   (d)   *Brown paper mask with string*

When they have decorated the masks in a fairly restricted way, suggest that they each do another one in any way they wish, or give them a character-type to portray.

Newspaper and adhesive tape   This is an excellent medium for a less able group and for all ages. No scissors are required as the paper tears easily; it is free and plentiful, and you can go on to invent costumes and sets from it as well. Simply suggest that everyone makes a mask, with eye holes, which completely covers the head but which can be put on and taken off easily without falling to pieces. Those who finish quickly can make a newspaper costume to go with their masks. Setting a time limit will encourage quick and spontaneous work.

Scraps and waste material   I had an interesting session with one adult group. They were asked to go out into the streets and collect any clean rubbish which would be suitable for making a sculptured mask. There were many small dress-manufacturing shops in the area, so they came back with a splendid pile of boxes, tubes from rolls of fabric, cartons, pieces of fabric, and packing tissue. We supplied two pairs of scissors, a staple gun, some adhesive tape and one pot of paint, and suggested that everyone should make a very simple, three-dimensional mask from the assembled material. The results were fascinating and varied. There was a huge effigy mask which would have looked marvellous in a carnival procession; a mask which completely deformed the body, as it had a covering attached to it which left only feet and arms visible; and another god-like mask suitable for use in a ritual.

Paint your partner   You will need sheets of sugar paper cut in half; enough large bristle paint brushes for half the group; some pins or a stapler; and paints (two colours) in enough pots for half the group.

The group divide into pairs, As sitting opposite Bs in a straight line. Everyone is then asked to fit a piece of sugar paper on to his head and secure it, so that it does not flop off, with either pins or staples. Once fitted, two small eyeholes must be made in the paper. The fun now begins. The As keep their masks on, while the Bs take a brush and a pot of paint and paint each feature in the correct place on their partners' paper-covered heads. A second colour can be added—for example, eyes, nose and ears in black and mouth in red. The painted masks are then carefully removed and put to dry, and the partners' roles are reversed.

Stick masks   These are hand-held, made from a piece of cardboard or plywood nailed to a stick. The cardboard or wood should be large enough to cover the outline of the head, and can be painted in any way.

A lip mask can be made in a similar way, and used when kissing is a problem. In one play we solved this by doing a send-up of a kissing sequence. The couple concerned each made two large red lips out of shiny paper and attached them to small sticks. At the appropriate moment the two protagonists presented their enormous shiny lips to each other and proceeded to simulate kissing to the beat of a tango rhythm. It was very lively and great fun.

Experiment and explore with masks as much as you have time for, using materials in various ways. Working with the group, you will invent some exciting effects. Think also about the effect of masks used by a chorus, or a group representing a crowd.

Improvising with masks

Mask work is fairly complicated and some groups do not respond well to it. It is therefore important to gauge carefully the right moment to introduce it.

Let the group form pairs. The procedure is similar to that explained in the 'Copying' sequence on page 13. A makes a movement, B watches; B then repeats the movement exactly. A must observe B carefully and try to decide whether the movement fits the mask B is wearing. A continues to experiment and to see how the mask moves lethargically, aggressively, and so on, or whether a more staccato type of movement would be more appropriate. Once A feels satisfied that the mask and the body movements are complementary, he can be more ambitious in what he asks his partner to do. Roles can then be reversed.

Development can be worked in groups of four. The two As are to be the master story-tellers and stand opposite their partners. (Remind them that the mask is able to communicate more powerfully when directly facing the audience; when wearing masks, students should always be discouraged from playing in profile or with their backs to the onlookers.) The two masters work out a simple, spontaneous story in movement. There should be no verbal communication between any of the four. The routine goes thus: A^1 makes a simple movement, masked B^1 copies the movement, A^2 relates his movement to the previous one and masked B^2 copies. A sequence of actions is learnt in this way by the masks. Once they have understood the mimed action, they familiarise themselves with it, and the masters watch to see that the sequence is clear. When ready, the group may like to share the outcome of their work. Roles can then be reversed.

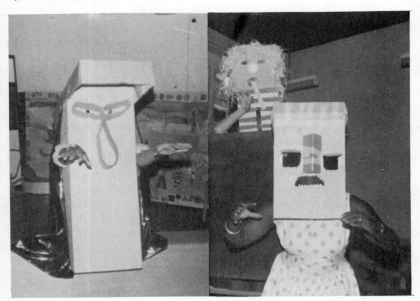

Overall mask   Painted paper mask

Paper bag mask   Paper sack costume

Film strip

Try this exercise before mask work, and then encourage the group to experiment with masks. Let them form small groups of four to six. They should all stand in a straight row facing forwards in a neutral position. Decide on a very simple action such as lighting a cigarette, drinking a cup of tea, or bending over to pick up a paper. As in a film strip, each person performs one part of the entire movement. Their movement must be carefully synchronised. For example, A moves his hand towards the cup, B picks up the cup, C lifts the cup towards his mouth, D puts the cup to his mouth and drinks, and so on. Timing is very important. Practice will be needed to find the most effective way of making four or five people look like one person drinking a cup of tea. Once everyone has acquired the knack of synchronising accurately, suggest that they use masks. It is particularly effective if they all make and wear the same kind of mask; you might use paper bags with identical features on them. I have found this exercise a useful lead into improvisation based on comic strips familiar to the group.

Mirrors and masks

The previous exercises evolved because there was not always a mirror handy when I was doing mask work with a group, or because too much confusion resulted when a whole group was wearing masks and there was only one mirror. If you feel you would like every mask wearer to work out the right movement without help from anyone else, you will need sufficient mirror space for each person to work on his own without being jostled or influenced by someone breathing down his neck. If you do find yourself in such an ideal setting, then let students find out for themselves how their individual masks move, react and respond. Give them time to find the right movement to fit the character which the mask imposes on the body. As this involves a lot of concentration and objectivity in front of a mirror, attempt this exercise with a mature group who can work unselfconsciously together.

Noses

A 'nose' session can be hilarious. You can either buy false noses from a toy store or carnival shop, or make them from cones of bright red or pink stiff paper, with elastic to go round the back of the head to hold the nose comfortably in place.

Allow time for experiment with the noses. How do they move, respond to each other, respond to a human being, react to other stimuli? I usually try to imply that they are a bit shy, stupid, obviously inquisitive, or easily frightened, but very affable, warm and friendly once they overcome initial qualms. This can be done by devious questioning while the group is exploring the movements and characters of the nose people.

Again, the group can work in pairs. A wears—and becomes—the nose, and B has to teach it to sit down on a chair, respond to an action, and so on. It is, of course, assumed that noses do not understand English and can only respond in very limited language. They can develop quite positive, cartoon-like characters on the lines suggested, and if later you dress them in old, clean sacks and add wigs made from string and hessian, a charming group of strange but lovable creatures will emerge who can be humorous as well as pathetic.

Extension—the nose shape can also become a beak shape and thus lead to bird movement. The movement needs to be directed in a different way, but this depends very much on personal experiment.

Creating simple sets

The sets I am suggesting here are made from waste or scrap materials and are very different from the conventional 'stage set'. They are very simple to make and should evolve from experiment. In a space such as I have described earlier in this chapter, you may use either a hanging set, provided the ceiling has batons, rafters or hooks which are accessible from a step-ladder; or a standing set, which must be stable and not likely to topple over at the slightest nudge.

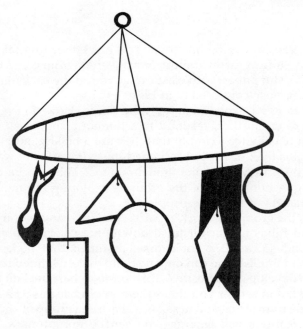

11   *Simple hanging set made up from various shapes*

Hanging sets

Drapes can be hung at different levels, made from muslin, plastic
sheeting, newspaper, carrot bags, huge sheets of brown paper,
newspaper and tissue paper, lengths of fabric, and so on.

Vertical columns can be made from chicken-wire or, better still,
from the cardboard tubes from inside rolls of carpet or linoleum, if a
local furnishing store can provide them. The columns can be
arranged in groups, or the set might consist of one solitary column.
Slightly more unconventional columns can be created from a string
of tin cans, motor tyres joined together with string or wire, hoops
strung together, or smaller cardboard rolls from lengths of fabric
(again, department stores are usually happy to give these away).

Screens can be made from rows of hoops tied together edge to
edge, or large posters made for hoardings, or rolls of white paper
(such as the end of a roll of newsprint, obtainable from a printer).

Experiment with picture-frame constructions, which may be
hung at different levels, some filled with tissue paper, or fabric,
useful for 'asides' to the audience.

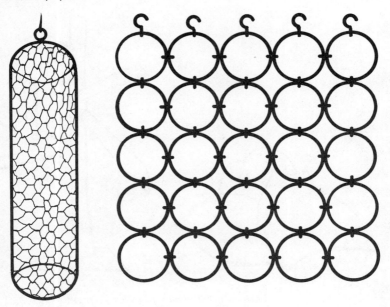

12   *Hanging set—chicken wire tubular construction*
13   *Hanging screen, made from wooden hoops joined together*

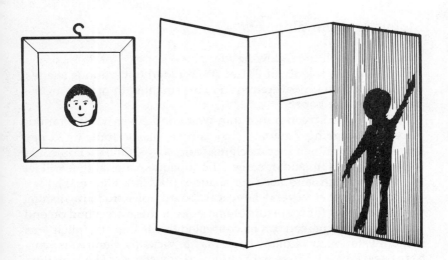

14   *Plywood picture frame, useful for period productions*
15   *Standing screen set, one end used for shadow play*

16   *Large stuffed plastic bags for floor set*
17   *Abstract standing set, made from fruit crates*

Mobile and standing sets

Experiment with the following ideas.

Chicken wire (plenty of it) can be moulded into various shapes; use it on its own, uncovered, or try covering it with muslin, newspaper, or tissue paper.

Make a triple screen out of thin wood and cover it with various pieces of packaging material—for example, plastic apple trays, egg boxes, cups from vending machines, and so on. One section could be covered with muslin or some other opaque material that will let the light through, and used for shadow play (see Figure 15).

Group together several large cardboard rolls from furnishing stores. Look out for remnants of linoleum; if these are stood on end still rolled up, a person can be concealed inside and the 'pillar' can move mysteriously. Collect large plastic sacks (cement bags, garbage bags) and stuff them with crumpled newspaper. They can then be grouped around the acting area and worked with in various ways.

Start a collection of simple items which can be bought cheaply (this requires adequate storage space). Look out for hat stands, wooden step ladders, office stools, bicycle and motor tyres. I have found that a simple wooden stand, as shown in Figure 17, is useful; it can be decorated in various ways, and can give an acting area an interesting focus.

Encourage the group to look out for and improvise around odd items they might find locally. One group I worked with painted an old iron bedstead white, and it inspired some very strong scenes which developed from improvisation. Eventually I was sufficiently persuaded, and it became an integral part of the set of a production called *Doors* (see pages 129–30).

If your group is very well disciplined and has a good sense of working as a team, then let the set be made up from members of the cast—for example, two players representing a door, a group balanced on one another to represent a high block of flats, one person as a ticket machine: plenty of scope for imagination and very simple, quick and striking. Jerzy Grotowski, in *Towards a Poor Theatre*, says: 'By his controlled use of gesture the actor transforms the floor into a sea, a table into a confessional, a piece of iron into an animate partner, etc.'

Props

On the whole, I prefer to encourage students to mime and imagine their props during a working session, but sometimes abstract or symbolic props can give added interest. It is worth while collecting a supply of odd-shaped pieces of wood, various boxes, and unusual objects such as pieces of metal piping, lengths of rope, and so on in a store cupboard. Realistic props do not stretch the imagination, and they can give a tatty look to a piece of work if they are cast-off or worn-out objects.

For an improvisation based on a period story or script I occasionally suggest realistic props such as a lorgnette, a fan, a snuff-box; each character might handle only one prop, to provide atmosphere, and costumes could be uniform and neutral in style with accessories (a ruff, frilly cuffs, skull cap, for instance) to give a suggestion of period.

If you are working towards a production, then do introduce the props right from the start (see Chapter 5). A prop can provide the stimulus for a scene, as in the exercises in the following pages.

Exercises with objects

Inventing with an abstract object—Sequence 1   The group sit in a circle. An object is passed round—it might be a piece of wood, a crumpled piece of newspaper, a box lid. Each person changes the character of the object as he receives it. It may either be passed from neighbour to neighbour, or taken to someone sitting on the other side of the circle. Try to encourage precise handling of the object, as the way it is handled demonstrates its identity and its transformation. Suggest that if A handles the piece of wood as if it were a pet rabbit, he must give B a rabbit rather than a piece of wood. B should accept it gently, as if it were a rabbit, and then change it into something else—say, an umbrella. B must then use the umbrella so that the transformation is quite clear, and pass on an umbrella to C, who develops the exercise accordingly.

Sequence 2—in pairs. Each pair is given an object (e.g. a box, pole, hoop, cardboard roll). A picks it up and turns it into, say, a telescope; B, noting the action, joins in the mime in any way which seems relevant. For instance, B might mime a pair of binoculars and a scene at the races might develop. Once the scene has been stated, A hands over his 'telescope' to B, and B turns it into another object (e.g. a lollipop). A then joins in, and they create another relevant scene. See in how many different ways the pair can use the object, and every so often let them exchange their object with another pair.

Sequence 3—The group explores the potential of a batch of objects all of the same kind, such as cardboard tubes, swatches of split cane, old tights, and so on. First, each person improvises with an object on his own; then each takes a partner, then the pairs make foursomes, and finally there is improvisation as a whole group. Exciting effects can occur if the group is sympathetic to abstract work. One group I worked with improvised a surrealistic type of meal using long cardboard rolls, another devised a human boat by linking themselves with stockings, and when we explored with swatches of cane a forest appeared.

The audience

Jerzy Grotowski, in his book *Towards a Poor Theatre*, reiterates my own feelings on present day theatre in the following passage:

'No matter how much theatre expands and exploits its mechanical

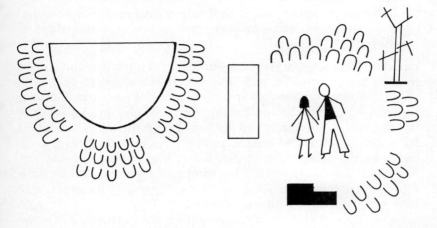

18   Ways of seating the audience
       (a)   Semi-circle
       (b)   Audience within the set

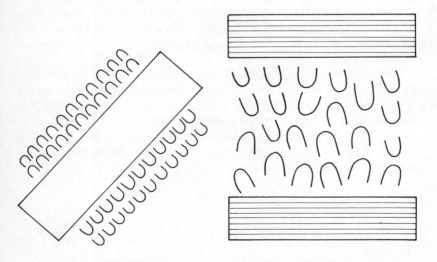

(c)   Audience on either side of the acting area
(d)   Audience having to change position

resources, it will remain technologically inferior to film and television. Consequently, I propose poverty in the theatre . . . for each production, a new space is designed for actors and spectators. Thus infinite variation of performer-audience relationships is possible.'

I much prefer audience and actors to be part of the action and am not fond of the proscenium-arch and picture-frame production. It is important that you should experiment and put your audience in a position which will be comfortable for them and the actors. It is usually best to discuss this with your group during rehearsals. I have sometimes had to seat the audience conventionally in a semi-circle, as the actors have insisted that the audience would not respond if they were obliged to change the direction of their gaze during the performance. But in a larger space and with a larger cast I have been able to experiment quite freely.

Figure 18 shows four ways of seating an audience; in (a) the audience is arranged in a comfortable semi-circle—this always works well, particularly if you can rake the seating. In (b), the audience is encompassed within the set, but as the main acting area is in the centre the actors must be aware that they are acting in the round most of the time. In (c), the audience is divided on either side of a central area; rostra could be used to heighten the acting area and a screen placed at either end. Figure 18(d) shows a scheme where the audience change their positions, concentrating on different ends of the room; the change could occur after the interval, if chairs were used, but stools would make instantaneous change possible. If you want to be really bold you could seat the audience on foam rubber on the floor.

An interesting experiment is to have the action very flexible: some of the time it is in the form of slides projected in one area of the space, then puppets illustrate a different aspect of the subject in another area, followed by the movement sequence, then film; and, throughout, improvisation is interspersed between the items. The audience needs to be limited in size and must be well shepherded by members of the acting group.

5   Preparing for a production

It is necessary for the group to have reached a particular stage in working together before they can attempt a production based on improvisation, or one which is a miscellany of material they have collected as a group. The following points might be useful as a guide to ascertaining their readiness to share an end product with an audience:

1 The group should be able to work co-operatively together, for without integration there will be no creation.
2 During the previous weeks they will have acquired some fundamental skills of verbal and physical expression.
3 With the exception of children under about ten years, the students should be able to 'become someone else' and thus to get under the skin of a character.
4 They will have some knowledge of stagecraft—creating sets and costumes from waste material, using a tape recorder, inventing sound, etc.

Paperbag animal masks and costumes

5 Most of the group will have acquired some insight into the way an idea or situation can be explored by looking at it from various angles. They can probe situations and reinterpret them in ways which are illuminating and revealing rather than static and clichéd.

6 There will be a strong sense of group loyalty, and a healthy respect for the teacher. The teacher must feel secure and also respect the ideas and opinions of all those within the group.

If the group have not yet mentioned a production, or the majority are reluctant, then I would advise you not to force them into doing a performance. Some groups gain their satisfaction and enjoyment from working hard on situations within a session, and feel no need to take the work any further. One teenage group I worked with regularly suddenly became production-conscious after two years of working together. The end-product was one of the most exciting I have been involved in, as their enthusiasm for performing for families and friends inspired them to work so hard and consistently in rehearsals that I had to devote much longer hours to the production than I had originally intended.

It is important that the teacher acts as guide and stimulus for the whole group. He should help them to produce a piece of work 'which strikes the imagination and makes observation a little richer than it was' (John Grierson), so that both players and audience participate in an experience which extends their insight and perception. I agree so much with Alan Bennett when he says that he wants 'to move people along a bit, so that they are not quite the same people when they come out of the theatre as they were when they came in'. Make sure, however, that you steer the group away from an over-intense and self-indulgent programme. Give them the opportunity to work out these feelings within the sessions. Let the end-product sparkle with pace, vitality and variety.

Choice of topic and audience

Start by deciding, all together, on the topic. It may arise from one of the sessions you have had, and will probably reflect the group's particular interests. It is important that it also provokes real interest from the teacher, as he is the one who must stimulate the group when they are sluggish and sustain them when they are slack. Discuss the various suggestions with them and consider the type of audience you could do the production for. Young children and

Animal masks

inexperienced students will probably prefer an audience composed of friends and family. A more experienced group of teenagers or adults might consider entertaining a local old people's home, youth club, play centre, or school; or they might like to do a piece of street theatre, in which case the topic could be connected with a community project or problem.

You can then discuss with the group the various ways of interpreting the topic. Is it going to have a significant theme? Will the production make a statement, and will this be relevant for the audience? Will the style of presentation be realistic, symbolic, abstract, surrealist, fantasy? Or will it include a combination of these ways of working? (If so, it will be important to co-ordinate them within the overall pattern.) Alternatively, will the group simply present a straightforward, imaginatively dramatised version of a story or situation? This is the best method with young children, but older students may prefer to explore the story and present it from an original viewpoint. You must decide, too, whether the group will work as a whole in developing a plot or situation or whether the members prefer to work as individuals contributing to the whole, working within a variety of small groups, sometimes with one person, sometimes with another. In this case, link items will be needed, or perhaps a song or movement item in which the whole group work together.

Whatever material and style of presentation you choose, your guidelines should be the ability of the group and the appropriateness of material and interpretation. Remember that almost any material or idea can be used with any age group (except the very young). Stories used even with toddlers may also be dramatised by adults, but the adults will obviously approach and present the work in a very different and more complex way.

What form will the production take?

The end product will consist of work which has grown from spontaneous improvisations based on the theme, idea or situation selected. These improvisations will need pruning and directing so that there is a structure for the players to work within when they present the idea to the audience. The team may contribute songs and poems which have evolved from particular sessions, to add an extra dimension to the production. Students working on this approach will usually want to experiment widely with ways of expressing an idea, and I have found that the resulting style is often physical and can be visually exciting. Other groups may prefer to examine a theme or story more academically. They will enjoy searching for suitable scripts, poems or passages of prose and deciding which to include in the format of the production and which are repetitive or irrelevant to the total concept. A programme can be made up from a miscellany of different writings supplemented by contributions from members of the team. I like to add a few scenes worked from improvisation, however, as this helps to keep the work fresh and spontaneous. It is also worth considering the use of slides, film or overhead projectors if you have the equipment, or can borrow it; if not, think of the possibilities of puppets, tape recordings and, of course, movement which can evolve from preparatory sessions.

In the same way, there is no reason why you should not explore an existing play text or script (for example, Shakespeare or a medieval Mystery play) and use improvisations to make the plot, theme and characters more relevant to the group. Then, instead of presenting the whole text, passages from it can be linked with scenes which have developed from improvisation.

Many people wonder if a group working on improvised drama should finally script the work and then learn their lines. I do not believe this is necessary or desirable if your aims are similar to those I

'I've had enough of this . . .'

have described. (Obviously, if you are using a poem or an existing piece of script, or the whole group is to sing a song, these elements will have to be learnt.) An element of improvisation is retained throughout the production if those taking part are never sure exactly what the other characters are going to say or do, and this keeps each player on his toes, sensitive to the others, and adds sparkle to the work. Unlike the actor working from a script, he does not have to rely on technique or simulate spontaneity. Also, if someone is absent from a rehearsal or ill during the performance, no one is let down. The group will have watched the absent player and will know the general idea of his role, and someone will be able to take over without much hesitation. During the final stages of rehearsal it is a good idea to suggest that people exchange roles and that the set is varied a little, so that there is still an element of challenge in the play. It is also interesting to ask the group to write comments on their work at the end of a performance; as you read them you will be aware of the variety of different interpretations seen by individual group members.

Preparation and rehearsal

If you are working in a school or within an organisation where other people are willing to help out with costumes, set, typing, and so on, involve them from the start. It is better to let them know your plans well in advance of the last hectic weeks of rehearsal, so that they can fit in the work you would like them to do with their other activities. It is also much more fun for the teacher to work with a team of people interested in the general organisation, rather than having to plead with colleagues and parents to help out at the last minute. If your building has a warden or school keeper, let him know about the production in advance, as late rehearsals and evening performances may mean overtime work for him. Even with a group as small as fifteen, it is helpful to have someone outside the team who can be relied upon to organise equipment, deal with programmes, hire a coffee urn, sort out expenses, and so on. If you have a very large cast—of a hundred or so—you are totally dependent on other helpers, so let them know from the start how they are going to be involved. I am eternally grateful to people who have committed themselves to productions involving them in hours spent over a sewing machine or dangerously balanced on the top of a step ladder.

Prepare a duplicated rehearsal schedule for cast and helpers at the start of rehearsal. Stress that it can change, particularly during the final weeks, and that they must check regularly the dates and times mentioned. Give the length of each rehearsal period. If you are going to need a whole day's rehearsal during the last week, warn people about this right at the beginning, give them the date, and ask them to arrange to be available. I've found that with sufficient warning all sorts of otherwise essential activities can be relinquished for this special event.

If you have an eight- to nine-week rehearsal period with a cast of about twenty, then arrange for one, or better still two, rehearsal sessions during the early stages. Stress to the cast that as everyone is concerned in the evolution of the production and in general decision-making, they cannot afford to miss rehearsals. The teacher needs to structure sessions quite carefully, delegating responsibilities as much as possible. Even young children are capable of accepting a little responsibility, such as making a props table, preparing drawings for the programme, or organising the tape recorder. For older children and adults you might divide your group as follows:

Designer and team responsible for visual effects—design and construction of the set, costumes, props, masks, etc. General co-ordination of all visual items.

Stage manager and team responsible for backstage and effects—lighting, sound effects; setting up improvised set for rehearsals; tidying and clearing set; checking in props on prop table. (See also pages 118–19.)

Front-of-house manager and team responsible for publicity, seating—programmes, tickets, posters, the press; selling tickets and programmes; arranging seating for the audience; tidying the room or hall before performances, opening and closing windows; providing coffee and biscuits during interval or after production.

In the final weeks you will probably need to introduce more rehearsals. For children, it also helps to make out individual schedules of work to be done (e.g. a list of costumes and props, to be made or brought by each person). Allow time during the week before the performance for:

  (a) setting up the structure of the set if it is a complicated one;
  (b) positioning the lights if there is a complex lighting plot;
  (c) editing the tape, if one is used;
  (d) arranging a technical rehearsal and all aspects of stage management;
  (e) cueing rehearsal, particularly for a complex programme; this helps both players and stage-management to feel more secure;
  (f) dress rehearsal, preferably involving everyone for the whole day;
  (g) a preview dress rehearsal for a specially-selected audience, prior to the first performance.

If the production involves children, see that their parents are warned well in advance and that they know the approximate duration of rehearsals.

Right from the beginning, stress punctuality, even during the initial working sessions. There is nothing worse than hanging round waiting for people to turn up. If you make a deadline for the completion of costumes, props and sets, keep to it. Try not to be soft-hearted, although it may be difficult.

If the production is to be for a large audience, start the publicity machinery rolling in good time. Delegate to your design and front-of-house teams the organisation of posters and tickets (printing takes time) and see that they inform the press, local radio station, churches, libraries, and so on. With a smaller audience there are not nearly so many problems. The lower you keep the costs of the production, the less money you have to recoup.

Stage management

I have always tried to encourage everyone in a group to be proficient at acting and at stage-management. In this way the person responsible for the lighting has a deputy who can take over when the lighting controller is needed as a player. A much better spirit of co-operation and co-ordination is maintained if each member of the group takes part in acting and is also responsible for some aspect of stage or front-of-house management.

Material

During the early weeks of rehearsal it is wise to accumulate and record as much material as you can. Delegate someone to make a list of the various items worked on during a session. Encourage the group to gather material from newspapers, books, photographs, records, and magazines, but warn them that it will not all be used. Stimulate them to write poems, passages of dialogue, songs, and collect these in a file. If you have a portable tape recorder, suggest that they record some interviews relating to the material.

You will also need to consider how the audience will be seated in relation to the acting area when working out movement, but at this stage nothing need be structured. Let ideas flow so that you have plenty to draw from when you come to fix the sequence of events.

Structure of the programme and sequence of items

You will probably need to start deciding on this about three to four weeks before the performance if you have a cast of about twenty. If, however, the cast is large, then the structure should be organised about six weeks before the final week.

The group and their teacher will select scenes which seem worth improving and working on, and which are also relevant to the theme or topic. There is no point in being sentimental and keeping a scene which has lost its original impact or which is irrelevant to the central issue; if you do this you will be sacrificing the effort as a whole. At this stage of the work you will have to direct quite formally the various items which are likely to be included. If you are working with experienced students, delegate some of the direction. Suggest that the co-directors consider some of the following points:

Where should the scene be cut and pruned?

Are the characters believable? Are their movements and voices consistent?

Do the players need to emphasise a particular point by careful phrasing or gesture?

Is the pace of the scene right?

Do the actions support the content?

Are the players familiar with the overall structure of the scene so that they can still improvise within the structure?

Is the scene visually interesting?

Are the players projecting themselves convincingly?

If the material has no formal plot, decide on an overall structure and then an order for the items within it. For example, you might consider a time sequence. In a production we evolved called *Patterns* (see pages 124–5), we started off the play in the early morning and worked through a day which involved seven characters who were travelling on the London underground. Once the structure had been formed, the sequence of items fell together quite easily. When a combination of source material is used (e.g. text, poems, songs, film) you need to consider the way in which each will relate to the theme and the total structure. If there are a number of short items which have, perhaps, been worked on in pairs, threes or fours, then continuity can be achieved with the help of 'links' involving the whole group (see below). The order should remain very flexible—you will probably find that additions and deletions will be made right up till the last few days of rehearsal. This element of change, as a production evolves, keeps the players on their toes and combats staleness. If people are absent during a rehearsal, others will readily step in as the missing characters. They should be quite capable of spontaneously improvising the dialogue.

Links

When working on a theme programme made up of various items, consider ways of linking these items, as already suggested. The links might be in the form of songs, or movement sequences, and will, if appropriately chosen, give strength to the structure. So often

I have watched a production which has been killed stone dead by an enforced break at the end of each item, particularly in dance and movement programmes; the scene finishes, there is a pause as the players walk out, the lights are dimmed, every one claps, and the set is altered before the next group of players file in and the action gets going again. The programme needs to *flow* and be a total experience. The material should be co-ordinated so that there is a balanced combination of movement, song, mime, say, as well as variety of mood and pace. It helps to have the whole cast sitting just outside the main acting areas, and as one section of the action finishes, the players involved can freeze and fade out as the next group immediately take over. Lighting can help considerably. If the action occurs in different parts of the room you can cross fade from one area to another (i.e., as the lights are dimmed in one area they come up on another). As long as the cast who are 'off-stage' move unobtrusively when picking up items of costume or props, they will not distract the audience's attention.

You might experiment with a chorus who appear at intervals and comment on the action (for example, a group of housewives, or travellers, or other supporting characters relevant to the scene); a narrator or group of narrators; a surrealistic sound or movement pattern; songs; slides, film, overhead projector. Remember to keep the links related to the immediate action and to the overall theme, so that they co-ordinate as well as illuminate the experience for the audience and keep people's attention primed and alert.

Costume—set—props—lighting

The costume, set and props should be co-ordinated so that there is a conclusive and appealing visual statement, rather than a hotch-potch of last-minute oddments.

I find it helps to make a series of lists, duplicated if possible so that each person can have one, about the details of costume for each character. This can be done for individuals, thus:

Character/ player's name	Costume	Extra items	Footwear	Props

or listed under groups or types of character:

Newspaper People

Costume: white tops, black tights, black shoes

Props: newspaper parcels, newspaper hats and other acces-
           sories; pram; masks for lunch-hour scene; fish and chip
           cones.

If duplicating equipment is not available, find a notice board and insist that everyone reads it at the beginning and end of each session. Suggest all come prepared with notebook and pencil.

Beg or borrow coathangers, iron, ironing board and long mirror, so that the cast can keep their costumes clean and pressed. There should also be a supply of safety pins, needles and thread, scissors, elastic bands and hair pins for last minute adjustments. Decide what is to be done about hair, and make sure footwear fits in with the rest of the costume.

Insist on a props table being made and use it during the last few rehearsals. Delegate someone from the stage-management team to be responsible for checking that each prop has been returned to the table at the end of a rehearsal or performance.

Aim to be scrupulous about the condition of the set. Is the general appearance of the hall tidy and clean? Have odds and ends of adhesive tape, paper, string been removed and chalk marks and pencil scratchings cleaned off? Is the structure of the set stable? If you are using rostra, do they need re-painting? Is the floor clean? A dustpan and brush and a mop and pail kept in a handy and visible place will encourage the group to keep the area spick and span.

The complexity of the lighting plot will depend on the amount of equipment available, so I have not gone into the intricacies of using lights. I suggest that you use a good text book, or, better still, have a few lessons from an expert. As a very general guide, aim for simple, clear-cut effects which help to turn on the imagination of both players and audience. Try to avoid a production becoming domi-nated by mechanism, which can so often go wrong and upset the spontaneity and concentration of the players. The purpose of light-ing is to illuminate the players and the action, create atmosphere and change of mood, and be an intrinsic part of the set. If you use coloured gels, treat them discriminatingly and bear in mind that they can transform the size and shape of the space, affect the set and costumes, create mood, atmosphere and patterns.

Audience

Check the fire regulations by consulting your local fire station. You may find that your premises are not adequately equipped for public performances and that you are only allowed an invited audience. You can, however, recoup some expenses by selling programmes and refreshments. You will probably need to purchase a fire extinguisher. Arrange for someone to make some large, clear 'No smoking' notices which can be placed in the room. Make sure that all exits are unlocked at the beginning of a performance.

Many a production has been marred at the opening by large, unmanageable programmes, so keep the size neat but make them interesting, informative and visually appealing.

If the production lasts about an hour, provide refreshments at the end, otherwise they tend to disrupt the performance. If the cast are willing to serve them to the audience, this makes the evening pleasantly informal as well as providing a chance for audience and cast to chat together about the work. If you do have an interval, try to avoid selling crisps and sweets in rustling paper which can be a terrible disturbance during the second half of the programme.

Above all, see that your audience is comfortable, so that total attention can be given to the action. Make sure that no one will be blinded by a badly-placed light, or disturbed by a whispering cast. The room should be warm but well-ventillated. Suggest that mothers with babies sit at the ends of the rows so that they can easily go out if the baby cries. A small audience is, on the whole, more satisfactory than an enormous one, as more care can be given to seating arrangements. There should be ample leg-room between rows and the chairs should be either raked or staggered so that everyone can see without fidgeting too much. I have found that it is much better to put on the show for an extra night than pack too many people into a small space. I have also found that in some places the audience react very noisily if the hall is immersed in total black-out before the play starts; it is better to cross-fade house lights and stage lights, so that there is never complete darkness.

Final rehearsals

It is worth establishing a warm-up routine prior to a rehearsal session, as this helps to relax the group, promote concentration, and limber the voice and body.

If the cast are particularly nervous, flabby or excited, introduce relevant games and exercises to combat these very normal signs of tension. Sometimes I have slightly rearranged the set before a run-through, and the group have had to adapt to the changes; or I've suggested that they have a complete run-through of the play but change parts. This demands extra concentration as well as being illuminating and refreshing.

Sometimes the teacher will need to feign severity if the cast begin to play up too much. A sense of discipline, preferably benign and motivated by the group, is essential for morale. At the slightest sign of giggling, admonish the cast freely. Warn them that it causes the audience and other players to suspend their disbelief and thus damages the entire play. It is also worth stating several times, to an inexperienced group, 'If a mistake is made, don't panic, just improvise in character to put it right, and no one will even notice.' Warn the cast, too, that if the audience laughs at a funny line or piece of action, they should pause until the laughter begins to fade, and then carry on. You will find that most players have an innate sense of responding well to an alert and sensitive audience.

Check and re-check the mechanical equipment (light bulbs, record stylus, etc.). I strongly advise having a second tape recorder on hand in case the main one fails, as can often happen.

If the cast is to be seated within easy reach of the acting area, arrange their positions so that exits and entrances are slick, and make sure that each player knows exactly where his props and costume accessories are placed. Remind the cast that as they will be visible throughout the performance, their attention must always be on the action.

Allow time during the last few rehearsals for 'the end' to be finally fixed. If you plan it too early, it becomes contrived and flat. So risk a last-minute decision and you are bound to get a good pungent finish.

Some points to look out for during final rehearsals

1 Is there still a lively element of spontaneity although the play is now structured? The cast should still have the opportunity to improvise within limits.
2 Is the pace keen, and the timing of exits and entrances precise? Are cues being picked up smartly? (Are players really listening to each other?)
3 Is each player really under the skin of his character? If not, you'll have quickly to help him by giving him some character exercises to encourage him to believe in the character more convincingly.

4 Can the cast be heard? Do the voices need to be firmer? (Perhaps a few simple voice exercises are necessary.) Are movement and gesture meaningful? Are the cast beginning to project as they work together?
5 Is there a feeling of overall flow and wholeness? (Are the links working?)
6 Is anyone still chewing gum surreptitiously? (Be severe!)

When watching the final rehearsals, I usually make cast notes divided into two sections, thus:

Comments for individual players	*General comments to cast*
Dulcie: clear mime, must try to enter more quickly.	Far too slow a start to song.
What about shoes?	Excellent movement.

When the rehearsal has finished, I go over the general comments, trying to make my observations positive, brief and, above all, encouraging. While the cast are tidying up I go round giving individual members their personal comments. This method helps to avoid a long dull monologue at the end of a rehearsal, and also keeps one directly in touch with everyone. You will find that individual chats to people help to keep a good, friendly working atmosphere. It is also worth going to the local pub or café with an adult group, after a session, or giving children coffee or a cold drink, so that you can all sit down on equal terms to talk together. I always give the cast a good injection of enthusiastic praise before they meet their audience, and after the performance I congratulate them all, as well as praising each person in turn. Praise is a tonic that everyone enjoys, so share it enthusiastically.

6   Synopses of some improvised productions

I propose to give here a very brief outline of some of the most enjoyable productions with which I have been closely involved. I hope these notes may stimulate teachers and their groups to explore new ground and experiment with new and unusual ideas. I shall always be grateful to the teachers who worked with me and to the children at Peckham School, London. They helped to evolve some very happy productions, and worked incredibly hard during school and, particularly, after school.

Today and yesterday

This arose from some drama work I was doing with a teenage group. We used to meet once a week for an evening session. Most of the boys had left school and were working in the area, some of the girls were still at school. I took over the group during my first year of teaching, and the programme evolved after we had worked together for two years.

The group very much wanted to use the stage and to hire lighting equipment, to which I agreed. The boys, some of whom were electricians, managed the control of the lighting board most effectively. The cast were dressed in dark casual clothes, and wore token accessories to indicate change of character or period. The scenes were linked by one boy playing a guitar and another wearing a mask and a huge sandwich board bearing a large sheet of cardboard on which the titles of the various scenes were written, and this acted as a programme for the audience.

The theme of the production was old age and youth—a universal problem and of particular relevance to teenagers. They explored ideas related to loneliness, relationships between young and old, a first job, a date followed by a meal in a restaurant; and, as they enjoyed working in the idiom of silent films, they mimed several items about a heroine, a hero, a villain and a railway line. Although the production naturally veered towards humour, there was a pleasant balance of mood. Two girls were determined to do the scene between Juliet and the Nurse from *Romeo and Juliet* so, after a lot of improvisation, they learnt the parts and made a fair attempt at performing it.

Patterns—an experimental fantasy

The Art Department at Peckham School were tired of decorating scripted productions, so they suggested that we should work with some of their material. They gave us great batches of paintings, clay rattles, masks, cane and muslin shapes, painted cardboard rolls and boxes, and we improvised extensively with them. A very talented group of about eight senior pupils were to be the key players, and the five drama groups we had organised after school were to form the rest of the cast, amounting to about a hundred in all. We decided that the lead characters were travellers in the London underground (subway), and the time sequence followed a morning-till-night pattern. Each lead character had a dream or nightmare during his journey. Once we had this framework, the play simply evolved as a result of good teamwork.

For the set we created a sort of circus tent, and used various levels: part of the stage, part of the well of the hall, and a sidewalk round the well (this was before the drama workshop was built). The audience sat in a semi-circle on rostra. We used many everyday objects for constructing the set, including wooden boxes, egg cartons, pieces of corrugated paper, fabric rolls, etc. In order to accustom the audience to abstract props, we had a warm-up in front of them. The oldest group were responsible for this, and called it a 'doodling' session. Besides a physical and vocal limber, they used some of the abstract props in realistic and amusing ways.

The travellers included an army officer, a drunkard, a baby-doll typist, a business man, a clown, a woman shopper, a deaf lady and a drop-out youth. They each wore a basic costume of bright tee-shirt and matching tights, trousers or skirt. Token accessories (e.g. military hat, scarf, collar and tie) were added, to denote each character's occupation.

The make-up we used was, for those days, pretty way-out. We coloured the faces with abstract designs using the brightest sticks of make-up we could find. For instance, the newspaper people had white faces with letters drawn on them, the machine people had squares and triangles of colour painted on their faces, and the main characters had a colour and shape which gave some indication of their character type.

Out of the twenty-one sequences within the structure, those described below were some of the most memorable for me:

The newspaper people, who started off as early morning commuters, then, wearing masks, became the lunch hour crowds and mimed the frantic search for lunch in a self-service restaurant. They next simulated the hurly-burly of the evening rush hour, and finally appeared as fish-and-chip eaters late at night. This was an excellent group, aged thirteen to fourteen, who contributed a great deal during rehearsal sessions and never let their work become set or stale. Each night they improvised something new within the structure of the situation.

The dreams, including the army officer's hunting-and-fishing dream; the cast in this sequence wore brown paper masks and dark clothes. They experimented with large swatches of cane in rehearsal and eventually a mime emerged depicting a fishing expedition and a hunting safari.

The clown got involved in a fight. His dream was a movement sequence inspired by the activities of a circus. The group depicting this wore white, loosely-cut trousers and white tee-shirts, and were given a very exotic, psychedelic make-up. The objects they worked with were the cane and muslin shapes mentioned above, which they wore on their bodies, heads or limbs. A rotating filter of coloured light gels illuminated them.

Machines dominated the business man's dream. This group, the machine people, invented some wonderful machine noises and movements. They dressed themselves in boxes—on their heads, arms and bodies. The episode was garish and terribly noisy, but had the desired effect of frightening the poor business man out of his wits.

The drunkard saw the tube station turn into a vast aquarium: the youngest group (eleven-year-olds) floated about as fish, seaweed, huge shells, weaving themselves into an ethereal sequence helped by lovely greeny-blue lights. We used a lot of polythene and plastic materials during this sequence, and experimented with all sorts of shapes made by the Art Department, some of which concertinaed in and out.

The underwater episode was followed, logically by the fish and chip eaters, who were brushed off the set by a crowd of loud-mouthed Cockney charladies. Other sequences included a street scene inspired by the stage instructions of *America Hurrah*, a clowning sequence involving a train approached by people carrying an impossible range of parcels just as the doors were closing, and a mime item showing advertisements coming to life to terrify a passenger.

As the programme was long we did need an interval. The Art Department organised an exhibition, and the visitors enjoyed drinking coffee and looking at the paintings and models made by the students.

Targets

As this was produced a few months after *Patterns* and before the building of the workshop, we tried to create a workshop atmosphere by placing both the audience and action on the confined area of the stage. We used a very simple set of rostra blocks and a back drop. Again, token accessories were used to indicate change of character or period, and a basic costume of tights and matching tops for the younger children and loose trousers and matching tee-shirts for the older ones. About fifty children stayed with us during the rehearsal period, which was surprising as we used text rather than improvisation.

As a theme, we tried to show some of the different aspects of childhood, using poems and plays written by, for or about children. We had about thirty items, ranging from authors such as Dickens and Yevtushenko to A. A. Milne and Bob Dylan and including items written or devised specially by the cast, and we tried to link them together so that one item glided smoothly into the next.

Nursery Rhyme Land

We organised this with the three lower school drama clubs. It was a fund-raising activity to make money for the still-elusive drama workshop. The main attraction was a visit to Father Christmas to receive a present. (The part of Father Christmas was superbly played by a parent.) Visitors had to make a thumb print and, after payment, were greeted by two huge effigy figures who took them to a tiny doorway through which, bent double, they entered Nursery Rhyme Land (this proved quite an obstacle for parents and the Mayor of Southwark). The Land was divided into areas where we concealed groups representing various nursery characters. As people approached, the characters came to life to mime out the actions of their rhyme or story. After this, visitors had to pass through the seabed where the Little Mermaid lived—we used polythene sheets and twisted them like a skipping rope as the travellers passed underneath, and soap bubbles were blown to add to the underwater illusion. They were then guided by the Ladybird to a fortune teller who told them how to get to Father Christmas. The next area was raised with rostra, and we hung curtains and sheets of thick wrapping paper so that it seemed like a thick, dark forest. This led to a sort of grotto, dazzling white, where each child was welcomed by a fairy and introduced to a magnificently bearded Father Christmas.

Dame Edith Evans at the opening of the workshop

Group mime at the opening of the workshop

Beginnings

When the drama workshop was finally ready and Dame Edith Evans came to open it, we organised two items. One group performed a piece in the main school hall which depicted how the workshop had been achieved, with a ballad written by the head of the English Department. In the workshop, three groups worked together to perform an experimental offering. It was based on an imaginative view of the piece of land upon which the workshop now stood, in

Doors: *teapot and cups*

Doors: *opening different types of doors*

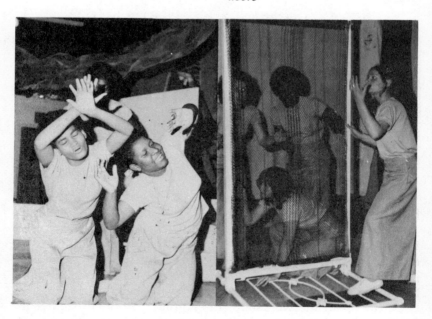

Doors: *storm*

Doors: *bedstead as a door*

three different ages—the past (dinosaurs and early man), the present (a teenage girl mesmerised by the pop scene, baffled by advertisements, and so on), and the future (with automation taking over and controlling people even when they rebel). It concluded on a positive note with a child finding a ball and, as she played with it, other children appearing to join the game. We used a large group of children and they were marvellous—they contributed so many ideas, and made us feel so confident that they would excel themselves on the day, that we did not 'set' the structure until the night before the opening. It turned out to be a piece of work which was very stylised and polished, and which puzzled a lot of the visitors who had expected a scripted item and not an ambivalent movement, sound and light show. Sadly, we had to prune rigorously as we were only scheduled to last twenty minutes. We were also programmed to perform three times each evening for three evenings, so that all those children, parents, staff and friends who had so valiantly contributed time and money to the building could have an opportunity of seeing the workshop at work. It was a hectic and vital week as we established ourselves in our precious new building.

Doors

This was a production we organised with a group of non-academic fifteen-year-olds. We used the workshop and had a cast of fifteen. The idea started from some thoughts we all had about the way people can be changed by entering or leaving a particular place. Eventually we wanted to find out more about the significance of all kinds of doors—doors to the mind, doors of memory, doors in a street, in a house—and the fact, too, that doors can be barriers as well as openings. The amount of work produced was staggering, and the involvement by the group quite exceptional. Some members of the group could hardly read, but when sufficiently encouraged they became articulate and perceptive. We worked very closely together and although there was no storyline we did portray various aspects of a street. These scenes were interspersed with other scenes related to the theme. Some of the items were very realistic, others surrealistic. An overhead projector gave programme details, and a second one provided illustrations for some scenes. We also used slides. The sources included nursery rhymes, children's games and newspaper articles, and provided some work of remarkable depth and insight. One of the poems I particularly enjoyed, written by Lyn Duggan, a member of the group, called 'The Door of Time':

That door, behind it, what is?
An actor, stern, cool and hard?
Looking into the mirror,
Into the reflection of his self,
to see the face, that time has moved?
Trying to find a part, of his face
that still looks young.
But, never will he find youth in that face.

This face of mine, I feel could stir,
If only I knew what to use,
Yes, this make up can change it.
Hide the cracks,
Cover dark patches.
But can it change me?
No! the door of time has closed!

The Black Light-Bulb

This was another production I enjoyed very much. This group were
excellent at doing absurdist work, and thrived on zany ideas, so we
evolved a play based on ideas concerned with the absurd: for
example, the usual becoming unusual, abnormal becoming normal,
situations in which objects grow large and humans grow small,
changes of relationship between people and animals, reversal of the
status quo, reversal of the expected, etc. It was a joyous programme,
and the group created some very rhythmic songs which lent themselves to excellent movement sequences. We also worked out a
system of complicated verbal and sound links to fuse the items
together.

By this time the Peckham workshop was being used to capacity,
thanks to a hard-working staff of three full-time and one part-time
teacher. Drama groups met after school every night and quite often
during the lunch hour. We organised a day during the summer term
when all the classes in the same year 'shared their dramawork', and
this became an annual event. It was not competitive. They enjoyed
improvising and then 'setting' a ten-minute production which had
to include a set, costumes and lighting, and some original work
emerged. The work was often linked to other subjects (history,
dance, religious education, English, art, for example). I shall always

be grateful for the contribution so many teachers made in helping the children rehearse and stimulating them to learn through drama which, I feel, is a method more than a subject. Besides the improvised work, we also produced epic scripted plays with huge casts, from which I learnt a lot about organising a production; I'm not sure whether the children learnt as much, for we were less dependent on their ideas. With large casts, too, it is difficult to keep in touch individually with all the people involved.

If you are in charge of drama in a school, club or community you must be able to cope with a hectic, packed programme of activities, involving all aspects of the work, and give everyone as much opportunity to do and to succeed as you can. Once the energy force has started to propel people freely, interest and ideas generate of their own accord. The more you do, the more there is to be done, and 'doing' is surely what drama is all about. As Hazlitt wrote: 'Man is a make-believe animal, he is never so truly himself as when he is playing a part.'

A course for teachers

Appendices

The story of Peter, Paul and Espen
(based on the Norwegian folk tale 'Per, Paul and Espen Askelad')

Espen was the youngest and smallest of three brothers; but he was the one who had to do the cleaning, cooking, shopping and any other odd jobs. He was a happy, friendly boy and did not worry too much about being bossed by his older brothers. Peter was the eldest; he should have had a job, but he was too lazy. Paul was next, and he was a bully. They lived in a small Norwegian fishing village with their old father, who was very weak and very poor and found it difficult to know what to do with his two elder sons.

One day a large boat appeared in the harbour, flying the King's flag. The villagers were very interested and left their work to go and look at the boat and find out why it had come to their village. When the boat anchored, the King's Royal Messenger came ashore with two trumpeters. They went to the steps of the town hall, and there the trumpeters blew four loud blasts, to the north, the south, the east and the west. Soon all the villagers, including the three brothers, were waiting for the announcement. The King's Royal Messenger unrolled his scroll and called out:

'The King has built a splendid new castle; but outside it stands a tree which blots out the view, and no one has been able to find a spring to bring water to the castle. Whoever succeeds in cutting down the tree and bringing water to the castle shall be given half the kingdom and the Princess's hand in marriage.'

The villagers were most excited, and did not return to work until the boat had sailed out of the harbour. Peter and Paul decided they must leave immediately for the castle. It was a long journey and would take two days. Espen was asked to come along to carry their belongings—poor Espen, the smallest and youngest but always the busiest.

The first day they travelled through a thick forest which was very silent except for the occasional hoot of a bird, or a swish as the wind blew against the fir trees. They would have to leave the forest before nightfall, because of the wolves; but Espen became aware of an odd sound, *Tk, tk, tk.*

'Peter, Paul, listen—what is that noise?'

'Foolish boy, it's only a woodpecker knocking on a tree. If you leave us to go and look, the wolves will eat you up.'

Espen wasn't afraid. He did so want to look. He followed the sound until he saw an axe hitting a tree. The axe stopped as Espen approached, and said, 'Espen, Espen, I've been waiting for you for a very long time. Please pick me up and put me in your knapsack. Don't tell anyone about me, and I'll help you like a good friend.'

Espen did as he was told, and then ran to catch up his brothers.

The next day the brothers came to the land of great rocks, stones and boulders. The rocks looked like huge and hideous trolls, and even Paul was afraid. But Espen wasn't worried. And then he heard another odd sound, *Ddd dng, ddd dng, ddd dng.* He didn't bother to say anything to his brothers this time, but went to have a look. Hidden behind one of the ugliest and largest rocks was a shiny spade digging away at the ground. When Espen appeared, the spade stopped digging and said, 'Espen, Espen, I've been waiting for you for a very long time. Please pick me up and put me in your knapsack. Don't tell anyone about me, and I'll help you like a good friend.' Again Espen did as he was told, and returned to his brothers. That night they slept on the bank of the river which led to the King's castle.

They woke early next morning and followed the river for a long way. Soon they came to a signpost near a bridge and, as neither Peter nor Paul had bothered to learn to read, Espen had to tell them what it said.

'To the castle—that way. And, oh! it says to the beginning of the river *that* way. I must go and see how a river begins!' said Espen. The other two, however, began to make their way towards the castle.

As Espen followed the river the other way he noticed that gradually it became a stream which grew smaller and smaller. Soon he saw a spring of fresh water spouting from the ground. He bent down to look, and as he did so he saw a shiny, shimmering shell lying on the green moss. He picked it up and put it to his ear. Then, to his surprise, he heard a voice like the sound of water: 'Espen, Espen, I've been waiting for you for a very long time. Please take care of me, and put me in your bag. One day you will need me, and if you shake me three times I'll help you like a good friend.' Espen gently put the shell in his bag.

When he caught up with his brothers they had almost reached the castle. Espen could see a crowd of people, and the big oak tree and, near it, the Princess, the prettiest girl he had ever looked at. The King looked angry, and was calling for silence. Then the King announced: 'You all know that whenever anyone tries to cut down this tree, two new branches appear in place of the old ones. No one else is to cut the tree unless he can chop it down in one go. Anyone who makes it grow bigger will have his hands cut off. So you had better all return to your homes.'

Peter and Paul were not going to be put off. Peter leapt forward with an axe and delivered a blow to the tree, but at once up grew two new branches. While he was dragged away by the guards to have his hands cut off, Paul stepped up and gave a huge swipe at the tree. He too was dragged off, kicking and shouting. While this was going on, Espen had removed the axe, spade and shell from his bag. He put the shell carefully in his pocket, and then placed the axe against the trunk of the tree. The Princess saw him doing this and burst out, 'Please, please, don't *you* be so foolish!' Espen smiled at her, and whispered to the axe, 'Chip and chop, chip and chop, little axe.' The axe chopped and chipped for all it was worth. Espen advised the watching people to move away, and in no time the tree crashed to the ground and rolled down the hill. Everyone was surprised, but Espen held up his hands for silence and said, 'I will now dig a well.' He put the spade on the hard ground and whispered, 'Dig deep down, dig deep down, little spade.' The spade dug and dug, deeper and deeper, until a hole was made. Espen then attached a long piece of rope to a stake, and slid down the rope into the hole. At the bottom, he took out the shell and shook it three times, saying, 'Bubble and flow, bubble and flow, little shell.' The water began to gush out of the shell as Espen climbed back up the rope.

The King greeted Espen at the top. Everyone cheered him, and the King ordered a great party to be held in Espen's honour. That day Espen was made a Prince. Do you think he married the Princess?—and if so, were they happy together?

(This story came from *A Time for Trolls—Fairy Tales from Norway* by Peter Christen Asbjornsen and J. I. Moe. I have retold it here in my own words.)

The Butterdish

This is an excerpt from a scripted play developed from improvisation by fourteen-year-old students (see page 83).

(The scene takes place in the kitchen. The wife is washing up; her husband, George, is reading the newspaper.)
WIFE: George. George. George.
GEORGE: Yes dear. Yes dear. Yes dear.
WIFE: It's broken. It's broken. It's broken.
GEORGE: What's broken? What's broken? What's broken?
WIFE: The butterdish. The butterdish. The butterdish.
GEORGE: The new one?
WIFE: Yes dear.
GEORGE: Take it back. Take it back. Take it back.
WIFE: Yes dear. Yes dear. Yes dear.
      Put on coat. Put on coat.
      Oh my face. Oh my face.
      Make-up.
GEORGE: Get new butterdish. Get new butterdish. Get new butterdish.
WIFE: Yes dear. Yes dear. Yes dear.
(Wife walks down the street carrying broken butterdish in a bag; she enters the supermarket where she bought the butterdish.)
WIFE *(quickly)*: I bought this dish only yesterday. I put it in hot water to wash, supposed to be strong but it went PIONGGG! And my George wants a new one. A new one. A new one.
ASSISTANT: I can't help. I can't help. I can't help. I only put out goods on shelves. Go to the factory. Go to the factory. Go to the factory.
WIFE: Where? Where? Where?

The wife eventually finds the factory. She first meets a worker who sends her to the foreman. The foreman is unhelpful and sends her to the Business Director three floors up. He is uncertain what should be done and suggests she goes to see the Designer on the fifteenth floor. She uses a lift. The Designer is very preoccupied with triangles, and takes little interest as he insists that it was not his design. She then goes to the Warehouse where she meets a very dim man, but he is able to find her another butterdish. She goes home triumphant. But alas, when she gets home the butterdish goes PIONGGG! again. George, of course, says she must get a new one.

Book List

Educational Drama

Drama Casebook: A Chronicle of Experience by John Challen (Methuen
Educational, London, and Northwestern University Press, Evan-
ston, Ill.)
Drama in Education by John Hodgson and Martin Banham (Pitman,
London and New York)
Drama in the Primary School by Janet Goodridge (Heinemann Educa-
tional, London, and Plays Inc., Boston, Mass., under the title
Creative Drama and Improvised Movement for Children)
Drama Guidelines by Cecily O'Neill et al. (Heinemann Educational,
London)
Drama Work One, Drama Work Two (2 vols.) by W. Martin and G. H.
Vallins (Evans Bros., London)
Development through Drama by Brian Way (Longman, Harlow, and
Humanities Press Inc., Atlantic Highlands, N.J.)
Exploration Drama by W. Martin and G. H. Vallins (4 handbooks and
a teacher's book) (Evans Bros., London)
Fifty Best Party Games for Children by A. A. Ross (Foulsham, Slough)
Improvisation by John Hodgson and Ernest Richards (Eyre Methuen,
London, and Barnes and Noble Books/Harper and Row Inc., New
York)
Improvisation for the Theatre by Viola Spolin (Pitman, London, and
Northwestern University Press, Evanston, Ill.)
Party Games for Children compiled by Mary Vivian (Foulsham,
Slough)
Remedial Drama by Sue Jennings (Pitman, London, and Theater Arts,
New York)
The Uses of Drama by John Hodgson (Eyre Methuen, London)

Mime and Movement

Mime – One, Two, Three by J. Dodding (Litho Arts)
Movement and Drama in the Primary School by Betty Lowndes (Bats-
ford, London, and Plays Inc., Boston, Mass., under the title
Movement and Creative Drama for Children)
Natural Dance by Peter Slade (Hodder and Stoughton, London)
Poems for Movement edited by E. Woodland (Evans Bros., London)
Teaching Mime by Rose Bruford (Methuen, London, and Barnes and
Noble Books/Harper and Row Inc., New York)

That Way and This: Poetry for Creative Dance edited by Frances Baldwin and M. Whitehead (Chatto Educational, London)

Theatre

An Actor Prepares by Constantin Stanislavsky (Bles, London, and Theater Arts, New York)

Building a Character by Constantin Stanislavsky (Methuen, London, and Theater Arts, New York)

The Empty Space by Peter Brook (MacGibbon and Kee, London, and Atheneum, New York)

New Theatre Forms by Stephen Joseph (Pitman, London, and Theater Arts, New York)

Seven Ages of the Theatre by Richard Southern (Faber, London, and Hill and Wang Inc., New York)

Techniques of the Stage Fight by W. Hobbs (Studio Vista, London)

Theatre in Education by John O'Toole (Hodder and Stoughton, London)

The Theatre of the Bauhaus edited by Walter Gropius (Wesleyan University Press, Middletown, Conn.)

Towards a Poor Theatre by Jerzy Grotowski (Eyre Methuen, London, and Simon and Schuster, New York)

Other Useful Books

Creating Children's Costumes in Paper and Card by Suzy Ives (Batsford, London, and Taplinger, New York)

Children's Games in Street and Playground by Iona and Peter Opie (Oxford University Press, London and New York)

Into the Life of Things: An Exploration of Language through Verbal Dynamics by Christabel Burniston (English Speaking Board, Southport)

The Language of Discussion by Frank Heyworth (Hodder and Stoughton, London)

Seven Themes in Modern Verse edited by Maurice Wollman (Harrap, London)

Simulation Games in Learning edited by Sarane Boocock and E. O. Schild (Sage Publications, London)

Voices (3 books and a teacher's book), an anthology of poetry and pictures, edited by Geoffrey Summerfield (Penguin, Harmondsworth). Also *Junior Voices* from the same publisher.

Your Voice and *Voice and the Actor* by Cicely Berry (Harrap, London)

Films I Have Found Helpful

('C' – suitable for children; 'A' – for teacher's use or adult students)
can be hired from:

Chinese Theatre delightful mime, all age groups.	Dr T. Olembert 15 Oslo Court Prince Albert Road London, NW8 7EN (Telephone 01 722 5656)

Three Looms Waiting—made by
    Dorothy Heathcote
    for the BBC programme
    'Omnibus' (A)
Explorations by Veronica
    Sherbourne
    movement for drama (A)
In Touch by Veronica Sherbourne
    a fascinating study of her work
    with mentally handicapped
    children (A)
The Fruit Machine by Christine
    Culbert (C, A)
	Concord Films Council
	    Ltd
	201 Felixstowe Road
	Ipswich, IP3 9BJ
	(Telephone 0473 76012)

Zoo—by Bert Hanstraa
    a humorous view of animal and
    human faces (C)
	Contemporary Films Ltd
	55 Greek Street
	London, W1V 6DB
	(Telephone 01 734 4910)

Man and Masque
    an interesting study of the way
    in which the Bauhaus group
    integrated art and movement
    (C, A); see also booklist
	German Film Library
	Viscom House
	6/7 Great Chapel St
	London, W1V 3AG
	(Telephone 01 734 9102)

Kabukie and *Noh Theatre*
    two interesting films, suitable
    for older children
	Japan Information Centre
	(Embassy of Japan)
	9 Grosvenor Square
	London, W1X 9LB
	(Telephone 01 493 6030)

Carmen and *Papageno* by Lotte
  Reiniger
  ten minute films of animated
  shadow puppets (C)

The British Film Institute
Distribution Library
81 Dean Street
London, W1V 6AA
(Telephone 01 734 6451)

The New Caribbean
  a marvellous look at the
  carnival in Trinidad (C, A)

Cable & Wireless Ltd
Mercury House
Theobalds Road
London, W1
(Telephone 01 242 4433)

Foreign films can be often hired from the Embassies of the country of origin. Local libraries and Education Authorities in Britain will be able to give advice about educational films available for hire.

Acknowledgments

This book would never have been written without the patience and encouragement of my parents, Kate and Leslie Stanley, and of my husband John Carroll.

The ideas in the book were mainly generated at Peckham School, London, so many, many thanks are due to the pupils and staff (particularly to David West) who worked so enthusiastically on the unscripted productions. I should also like to thank my colleagues in the Inner London Education Authority who have always been such a support, and particularly Mr Geoffrey Hodson and Miss Maureen Price who organised those splendid drama courses when I was able to work with some inspiring tutors, including Brian Way, Gavin Bolton, Collette King and Veronica Sherbourne; also Saber Sohby, David Huggett, Tilak Shanker, H. Widdows, David Carter and David Brinson for the photographic illustrations, and Kate Buxton who drew the line illustrations.

1980   *Susan M. Stanley*

The poem 'The Chant of the Awakening Bulldozers' (page 78) is reprinted by permission of Atheneum Publishers, New York, from *Catch Me a Wind* by Patricia Hubbell, copyright © 1968 by Patricia Hubbell.